JESUS, TEACHER AND HEALER

JESUS
TEACHER AND
HEALER

from White Eagle's teaching

THE WHITE EAGLE PUBLISHING TRUST

NEW LANDS · LISS · HAMPSHIRE · ENGLAND

White Eagle's teaching comes through
the instrumentality of Grace Cooke
The editorial matter in
this book is by Jeremy Hayward

First published October 1985

© *The White Eagle Publishing Trust, 1985*

British Library CIP Data
White Eagle. (*Spirit*)
Jesus teacher and healer: from
White Eagle's teaching
I. Title
133.9'3   BF1301
ISBN 0-85487-065-2

*Set in 11 on 13 point Baskerville by
Goodfellow & Egan Phototypesetting Ltd, Cambridge
and printed in Great Britain
by Oxford University Press*

CONTENTS

I

Jesus the Christ

WHENEVER White Eagle spoke, he had a remarkable way of conveying more than just words. While talking very simply, he would seem to bring an awareness of what lay behind the words. He would not dogmatise. So often in his talks it would seem that his real purpose was first of all to give. He would bring a blessing. He would make his listeners feel that they too were part of a world of light, and of love, that was wider than that of everyday life – and yet not separate from it. In so much of his teaching he based what he had to say on the life and philosophy of Jesus; and it was perhaps when he spoke about the figure of Jesus that he seemed to have least concern with mental argument, but would above all, and simply, bring a quality of love to the heart. He would love. He would not try to persuade his earthly brethren to follow a particular line of thought. However, in the light that he brought one would realise that he was also speaking to what he would call the higher mind.

It is this spirit that informs this book. Perhaps too the way he speaks is a beautiful discipline (if that is the right word) at a time when so often the purely mental faculties are disproportionately developed. Surely White Eagle's great gift to us above all is that he helps us just to draw close to that wonderful figure of the Master, so human yet divine.

White Eagle's picture of Jesus really emerges through the whole book. This first chapter, however, prepares the ground for what is to follow. It introduces extracts from White Eagle's teaching, in all of which he is talking about the life and mission of Jesus, but which together give a conception of what it means to speak of Jesus *the Christ*. Although quietly given, they begin the work of the whole book, to realise a new vision of the mission of Jesus, for the New Age.

Here are White Eagle's words:

We bring to you all love from our world of light. And we pray that it is not only in the words we utter that we shall bring to you the message of the higher worlds, but we hope to impress your souls and your spirits with the power from the world of light and love.

When he has passed through what we can only describe as the intermediary stage after the death of the body, the first thing which man in his spirit becomes conscious of is an overwhelming feeling of love. This is truly the awakening of every soul, although it may not occur immediately after death, for all depends upon the life and the degree of spiritual evolution of the individual. But always, after passing through a process of cleansing, and after the growth in the individual of a sense of humility, does the soul awaken to a world of beauty and love. We come back in bands from this world to bring to your consciousness the feeling of divine love.

Nearly two thousand years ago one of the Great White Brotherhood came into incarnation with a mission above all others, as a teacher and revealer of the love we speak about; the love upon which man's whole life is to be built. Through Jesus flowed the heavenly light, the Sun, the supreme light of the heavens. In your world you know that light by the name of Christ; and as this light came through the prepared channel, and Son of God, Jesus, you know this great one as Jesus Christ.

Today, many people reject any idea of the saving grace of Jesus Christ; and we hope to make clear the real meaning of these words.

Christ is that light which has manifested in degree through other teachers. The mission of Jesus was to bring to humanity the teaching of love, because all human development and development of the earth itself is based upon the common denominator, love. His message was very simple: 'Love one another'. Love is the fulfilling of the law. Love in man's heart is his saving grace. It is not the man Jesus Christ as a human being who saves the world; and yet, on the other hand, he is a saviour, because through

3

him came this message, and his was an example of divine love demonstrated in human life.

Jesus brought this message not only in regard to man's material life, but for the development of his spirit. So many men in the past, and indeed today, have had little knowledge of spirit-consciousness. Yet this consciousness is implanted in every living being. You all have it – even if it be a spark almost smothered by the mind and materialistic thought.

One of the purposes of the message of love which the Master Jesus brought, and which we are trying to voice, is that love is necessary for the unfoldment of spiritual gifts. Without love you cannot get perfectly true spiritual contact and spiritual communion.

The incarnation of Jesus Christ took place at the beginning of the Piscean Age, the age of the emotions, when humanity was developing and growing emotionally. Now we come to the Aquarian Age, when along with the mind the emotions are again being worked upon, but at a higher level; and this means the development of a sixth sense in man, which some people call intuition, meaning a sense or awareness of other levels of life beyond the physical. Before you can make contact with higher worlds you have to develop a sense which can respond to their vibrations – let us say that you have to adjust your own radio set to the required wavelength! Your personality is the radio set, which can be attuned to different levels of life or consciousness. It must in fact be attuned to the basic law which governs your receiving set – the basic law of love.

Christ, through Jesus the initiate, brought this message to your world. Love is the saviour. In earthly language it has been said, Jesus Christ is the saviour. Yes, but it is the divine love and intelligence behind the Christ-consciousness which is the saviour of the world. But also each man has to learn to be his own saviour by developing a consciousness of Christ in his daily life.

The real, the true proof of eternal life and of the higher worlds lies in the heart of man; and this is why Jesus taught love, because love develops the heart centre. The symbol of man's heart centre is the astrological symbol of the Sun. You cannot live without the Sun. You cannot live without your heart beating. The centre of your universe is the heart-beat of all life, and the Sun represents love.

Love is the goal of that new age of blessedness, brotherhood and beauty which surely, surely follows after the days of preparation and struggle. You will get there. Look up and strive, and all the angels in heaven will be with you. God bless you, every one!

*

In his teaching White Eagle makes a distinction between Jesus, the great Master, and the Christ, that greater light which is not limited to one human being, but for which he above all was a channel. But although other teachers in their own way have reflected this Christ light, White Eagle has often spoken of the supreme mission that Jesus had, and of the baptism that he brought to the earth:

The elder brethren who come to serve humanity from the spiritual level of life have a deep love which few men can understand, but which man can still *feel* to a certain extent. For every man can respond to the love from the spiritual worlds – from his companions in spirit, and from those whom we may call the saints and the elder brethren; and, above all, from the great light, the Christ light . . . which at the Christmas season you worship in the form of the Christ child.

The 'light which lighteth every man' has always been known to the mystic as the 'saviour', and the 'Son' of God. Christmas is therefore a festival of rejoicing because of the rebirth, the apparent rebirth, of the Son.

The record in the gospel of St John says that this Cosmic Christ came to earth and manifested through the flesh. You are told too how Jesus the initiate was born as a little babe. His mission was to prepare a physical vehicle for the incoming of the glorious Christ spirit, which came as a shaft of light from the heavens and later manifested through the body of the great initiate Jesus. We would emphasise the wonder that so great a spiritual glory as this can manifest through God's creation, man: a glory which is not limited to any one channel, but can eventually shine through the whole human race — that is, when it has prepared itself for such an incoming. Christ is the Sun of life. Christ is the glory of human life.

We would emphasise the great sacrifice of the Lord Jesus. All souls that voluntarily come into matter to help mankind make a very big sacrifice which earthly people take for granted; they think that the elder brethren voluntarily come back to earth to help them because it pleases them. It is true to some extent; those who come back to earth because of their intense love of mankind are blessed with a joy and a happiness beyond all earthly comprehension — but they come not for that reason. They come, brethren, because their love is so great.

Jesus had a particular mission to bring to this earth. At the time of the Christ initiation or crucifixion of the man Jesus there was a flooding of the whole earth with light. It was more than just a passing out of the physical body and the great demonstration that man's spirit is triumphant over death; through Jesus' crucifixion there came a baptism of the whole earth, the soul of the world, with the Christ light. This is why Easter is not sorrowful but a time of inexpressible

joy. The joy which you are able to feel at Easter-
time is due to the fact that through this festival
you are able to touch and respond to the outpouring of love from the great Christ heart.

*

Through Jesus' great self-surrender in the
crucifixion*, there came a bathing of the earth
with the radiance of the Christ light.

As we read White Eagle's words, we may ponder
on the phrases 'Christ is the Sun of life . . . Christ
is the glory of human life', and 'You are able to
touch and respond to the outpouring of love
from the great Christ heart'. When White Eagle
speaks of the Christ in this way he touches on a
great mystery that is really beyond all human
comprehension. For although to us the Christ
light, the 'first born of the Father', is a universal
spirit, beyond all thought, this great light is not
apart from human life and love. The Christ
manifests through form; in a mystical sense,
through human form.

White Eagle once touched on this great mystery
of the Christian revelation when he said:

We have often referred to the Son, Christ, the
Golden One. Think of the Golden One as being

---

*Perhaps we can conceive just a very little of this great
flooding of the earth with light through Jesus' utter self-
surrender in the crucifixion, through the stories in the
Acts of the Apostles of the wonderful light and power in
which the early Christian brotherhoods were uplifted.

in the Sun, the spiritual golden Sun, the essence, the life; the Creator in the Sun, but who has taken form as man. This is difficult for earthly man to comprehend – but the form, the face of man is (or can be) the most beautiful of all God's creations. You may think then of Christ the Son as having the most heavenly, most wonderful and perfect face; similar to that of humanity, because Christ is in humanity, and is a part of humanity. This is a mystery which so few can comprehend at present. Nevertheless, as the soul rises plane by plane and sphere by sphere into the heavenly life, these mysteries will be unfolded, as the rose unfolds its petals beneath the warmth and light of the Sun.

White Eagle says that not only by his self-surrender, but by his whole mission Jesus revealed in all its fullness the divine spirit that dwells in and can illumine every human heart. When he talks of how the Christ spirit dwells within every man, he speaks not in complicated or elaborate language, because (as he says in the ensuing talk) words can so often deaden; but rather, so simply – as if he were leading us to the silence of our own hearts. The talk from which this passage comes really brings us to the centre of his whole message. It opens by taking up a theme that has already been established:

We do not think of the Son of God quite as our orthodox brethren do: when we say the Son of God, we do not limit our meaning to Jesus the Christ. We recognise Jesus as a great Master, one of the brotherhood of the light, who was highly evolved and attuned to the first-born of the Father–Mother God. What is the first-born of God? 'God said, *Let there be light*: and there was light.' And it is the light which brings forth food, both spiritual and physical. Without the light you would die, both physically and spiritually. The light is the first-born, is Christ the Son of God.

We are hoping by our explanation to bring to you a clearer understanding of the simplicity and the beauty of holy communion. Jesus demonstrated what he meant by communion when he called together his disciples, and shared the bread and the wine with them. The wine is the symbol of the spirit, of divine essence within the heart of every man on earth. But when man is young in spirit he does not recognise the essence of life, which is *love* – just simply brotherly love and kindness and gentleness.

The Master Jesus, the great healer and truth-bringer to mankind, demonstrated the truth of the power of the Christ in man by his healing of the sick, by his raising of the dead, by his comforting of the mourner and the sorrowing. He raised *all* those with whom he came into contact

– he raised them from their sorrows, from their sickness, by giving them the Christ spirit in him; in other words, by sharing with them the bread and the wine, the holy communion, he stimulated in all his listeners the growth of that living golden seed of light which is in the heart of every man. This, my brethren, is the white magic which heals, which brings order and happiness out of chaos and sorrow.

We are trying to convey to you all, in our simple words, the power of the light, of the universal Christ love. Jesus said: 'I am the light of the world'. the I AM is the seed of God in man's heart; it is the light; it is the still small voice which speaks in every human heart. The I AM is Christ, the universal spirit of love, which speaks through the heart of all good true men and women.

If you learn to listen to the inner harmony within your heart you will know that you are enfolded by a company of shining sons and daughters of God. They are in their temple of light, or in the heaven world, the world of spirit, of eternal life. They reach down to help their younger brethren to rise in spirit into that eternal world of love and perfect brotherhood.

We draw your attention to the picture, the symbol of the communion table. On the altar is the symbol of the holy grail, in all its simplicity, the grail in which the light burns. In spirit, draw near to the table and feel your at-one-ment with the Lord your God. And let the symbol of the holy grail and the little flame remind you that this is the light in your own heart – the light, the divine essence of life, the infinite and eternal love.

There is no death. The body falls away as an old dress, but the spirit which is the Son of God can never, *never* die. It is our work, your work and ours, to kindle that grail light in the heart of your fellow beings, not by words (for often words kill it) but by the spirit, the love in the heart, which gives eternal life.

This is the truth which will redeem the world. Be patient, and as you have heard us say so often, keep on quietly, keep on quietly, because it is through the quietness of the heart that the light radiates throughout the whole of creation.

We leave you with the words of our ancient brethren: peace be with you and love enfold you and sustain you.

*

It is the great work of man's life on earth little by little to develop and unfold this Christ spirit; this is a selfless work – but through it man rises by slow degrees into the inheritance of his true life. Although all the great teachers have shown to men the life of the spirit, according to White Eagle Jesus supremely revealed to man the Christ life in all its fullness; indeed, through his great surrender and sacrifice he brought to mankind, in a way beyond our comprehension, a great initiation into this higher life. White Eagle says that the tearing of the veil in the Temple at the time of the crucifixion was a symbol of the opening of the way to the true Christ-consciousness for all men (the consciousness which White Eagle would point us to in the beautiful extract just given).

The great teacher whose simple love has inspired so many, countless, souls, is still at one with human life, White Eagle says, not only bringing healing and comfort, but pointing the way and saying for all men and women, 'I and my Father are one'. Again we touch on a profound mystical truth in simple human form:

The soul of man has to learn to develop and uplift the Sun within him through human experience. Jesus came to bring this message. He brought to humanity a light which is inconceivably more lovely than the physical sunlight of Spring. He carried it with him throughout his earthly pilgrimage; and he revealed this light to his disciples when they were raised in consciousness, when they had withdrawn from the noise and clamour of the world. They were a waiting, silent brotherhood. They saw the glory of his spirit at the time of the Transfiguration. This was a demonstration to the man of earth that he was a

Sun-man, a man of light. Moreover, he beautified the lives of all who came near him. He lived to heal, to comfort and to illumine.

Today Jesus appears to be very remote to most people; they think only of the figure of the historical Jesus of long ago. Only a few understand how near is the human presence of this universal teacher, that he still heals and raises men into the consciousness of his heavenly Father.

We would raise you up so that you can conceive of his presence. Can you imagine the Christ Temple in the heavens? Can you conceive of the perfectness of this life? Into this Temple, into the great circle of white-clothed brethren comes he whom you know as Jesus, the carpenter's son. He is so simple, so pure of spirit. He radiates purity and simplicity of life. He says, 'I am the carpenter's son. I have to execute perfect work with the tools and the material handed down to me by my Father. I am the example of the perfect craftsman'. There follows a great silence. The truth strikes into every listening heart, for he says, 'Be ye perfect, even as your Father which is in heaven is perfect'.

*

These opening pages have introduced the vision White Eagle gives us of Jesus as the revealer of the glory of the Christ light. He has also spoken on several occasions, and in different ways, of the earthly life of Jesus. He has, for instance, touched on Jesus' link with the Essene brother-hoods:

We are thinking of the Master Jesus, whose last incarnation you will celebrate at Christmas time. We cannot adequately paint in words a picture of his glory, his gentle and gracious spirit.

Jesus the Master was not of this earth's life-stream. We mean by this that Jesus of Nazareth was much older than this earth. He had been through experiences of a very exalted nature in preparation for his mission, the full power and implication of which is yet to be realised by people on earth. The Master Jesus was a pure soul who had unfolded the inner glory. He came down from highest heaven to this earth plane step by step and took upon himself various forms, bodies. All his incarnations were leading up to the appointed time when he would take the great incarnation which would radiate light and blessing; for the spirit of Christ manifested through Jesus of Nazareth in greater degree than it had ever manifested through any other master or teacher. This was the culmination of the Christ power which was and is to flood the earth and all mankind.

Think for a moment of that pure soul who came from the highest heights, the heaven world

15

most remote from earth . . . He came down to prepare the way for the manifestation of the highest, the Son.

Jesus of Nazareth was trained in the Brotherhood of the Essenes, who taught the unfoldment of the inner light, who served the community in simple ways, tilling the soil, weaving, doing carpentry and all manner of handcraft – brethren with great love and gentleness in their hearts and lives. From this community the Master Jesus came. He was trained in early days by wise men, although little or nothing is told in your bible of his early years, except of his going to the Temple. Here we would draw your attention to the implications of the young boy being taken by his parents to the city, and entering the Temple, where he talked to the men of learning. They were astonished at his wisdom, because he spoke as one who had come from a far land, as one having acquired great knowledge and great wisdom.

As was the custom, he would have worked with his hands, as did all the brothers. He was not a carpenter quite as you understand it, but worked with wood and stone. He was prepared both spiritually and physically to be the physical vehicle through which the glory of Christ would come.

The mystery which we are endeavouring to teach is this: that man is glorified by the Christ spirit, and the purpose of man's life is that he shall glorify the flesh and glorify the earth.

*

When White Eagle has talked of the personality of Jesus, he has stressed the simplicity which his soul had attained. 'We are reminded of this sweet, pure love and of his spirit which disliked hypocrisy; his spirit which was pure, gentle and all love. Meditate upon his character, upon his teaching.' White Eagle once described the love of an elder brother in a way which may give us just a fleeting glimmer of the love of a soul through whom the Christ light was revealed and shone:

Now, let us gaze upon the perfect form of an elder brother or Master. What is the impression made upon us as we gaze upon it, this perfect form? Oh, such gentleness, such love! Can you conceive the purity and loveliness of the master soul? Can you see the expression, shining with love – not weak or tepid – a love which is strong and eternal, a love which serves, a love which is wise, a love which can withhold as well as give? Now, hold this picture, my brethren, of a master soul . . . feel the wisdom, the tenderness and the gentleness of the Mother, together with the strength, the power, the courage of the First Principle, the Father – the dual soul – and see this soul with power to watch over all mankind.

17

Almost impossible as it is for the human mind to grasp, we would indeed endeavour to convey to you this sense of loving care in which you live and have your being.

*

Finally, although we have seen how White Eagle speaks of the glory of a soul such as the Master Jesus, he also says that we are wrong to think that the life on earth of any illumined soul is somehow in a category apart from our own. Such lives show us what it is to be human:

We have referred to the joy in the life of the Master Jesus. You do not possess a complete record of his earthly life, or of the life of other souls who have attained mastership, so you do not know the spontaneous happiness these Masters have enjoyed. The Master said, 'He that believeth on me, the works that I do shall he do also; and greater works than these shall he do'. Do not think of the Masters as beings apart from ordinary people like yourselves, but think of them as your elder brethren, as souls who have learnt the required lessons, who have attained a high degree of mastery first over themselves and then over the physical conditions of life. Above all, they all found the joy of life. It is such a temptation to think that it is easier for other people to be good than it is for you, or that your circumstances are more difficult than those of your neighbour. Do not think that you are any different from those who have attained mastery. For you are treading the same path as they have trod, and are here in the body for the same purpose. We draw your attention to the symbol of the winged disc, or the winged beast such as the sphinx. The wings symbolise the power within every soul to rise above its physical nature and material conditions. Every living soul has wings, and will in time learn to use them.

Many people today do not like the idea of a mediator between themselves and their God. They like to feel that they go direct to the God-head. They accept the truth of God as an infinite being, a divine intelligence which orders all things; but do not associate that divine intelligence with any human being, thinking that this limits their conception of the infinite power they worship as God. Yet all souls in the end come to realise their need for a spiritual teacher, one greater and wiser than themselves, who has trodden the same path and therefore can point out the way. Man feels the need for a teacher, one like himself, one who understands his weakness, his weariness, his ignorance, one who loves him. Through such human and divine love man is himself lifted up to mastery. The only way to attain to this high degree is through a life controlled and mastered by love, a love which contains all the virtues of the Master.

This is not easy, but it is your path. You may delay the process for a few incarnations if you like, or you may make a supreme effort in one incarnation and travel far; but so long as you delay, you suffer pain, sorrow and weariness. But whether you delay, or whether you move forward now, remember that the Masters, and particularly the supreme Master, come to humanity to help all souls to attain freedom, to attain mastery over the weakness of the flesh. The Christ-circle in the heavens draws very close to the earth. From that circle of light and power, light comes to the earth to help mankind. It is for man to respond to that gracious love which is seen manifested in the lives of the Masters. The Christ-circle in the heavens is waiting to help you; you are no different from any other soul; you may respond to this outpouring, and by your response help all others whom you contact. This is the way of life. This is the purpose of life. It is not enough for the soul to await escape from earth to know this perfect life. It must be lived and known by all humanity whilst still on earth.

Let us look then towards the Christ-circle. Open wide the heart to love; then the wings begin to beat and man rises from earth to heaven.

II

Divine Law working in Human Life

On Miracles

WE WOULD like to talk with you in a very simple way about the miracles of Jesus. We ourselves find within them a beautiful mystical interpretation, but on this occasion we would emphasise the truth of the actual material manifestation of these miracles.

Will you to begin with remember the miracles which take place in nature every season of every year? A little brown seed is planted in mother earth. Surely it is a never-ending miracle when that little seed bursts its shell, grows into a plant, and produces exquisite flowers, beautiful perfume and luscious fruit to sustain the physical body of man. You can see the miracles of nature taking place all about you, although you are so accustomed to this that it seems perfectly ordinary to you.

Is it not also a miracle when, having laid aside the physical body, a beloved friend is able to make you aware of his love, even to communicate to you certain facts, proving to you that he lives

21

on beyond death of the body? Surely a miracle? Yes, but it is also a demonstration of spiritual law – not a psychic, but a spiritual law.

Let us now turn to think of the perfection and the beauty of the soul and mind of the great Master Jesus. Let us think of the beauty and the love which he always radiated, and his teaching: 'Thou shalt love the Lord thy God with all thy heart, and with all thy soul, and with all thy mind. This is the first and great commandment. And the second is like unto it, Thou shalt love thy neighbour as thyself'. The words are so familiar! But to love God, with mind and heart and strength and soul . . . how many come within miles of so loving? Men and women while on earth so rarely know the secret of this love. You have so often asked us, 'How do we find this secret, White Eagle?' To love God is to be at one with him. When the mind is clouded with the confusion of materialism, and subject to the claims of the physical body, when the physical body and intellect clamour constantly for attention – it is not easy for man to *be still and know God*. You can and will attain to it, but it requires strength of purpose. God is not reached by one who says 'Oh, I can't do it – I've tried again and again and again, and I just can't do it – it's no use'. Beloved brethren, you do not feel thus if you seek God correctly.

Most men and women on earth think that the

personal 'I' is the real 'I', and feel it their duty to develop and strengthen that 'I', to enhance its importance. But when, perhaps in meditation, you have experienced, if only for a flash, an awareness of God and the peace which floods your mind and your being with light, then you have touched the real 'I' which dwells within and which is at one with God, the Father; you are illumined by that little flame which is part of the one great light. You may not be able to sustain such a moment of illumination, but having touched it in a flash, you have accomplished much. The way is to be still . . . be still. We cannot emphasise too strongly the importance of trying to make this contact, for it will help you forward in this life and in those other lives on earth which lie ahead.

We would also say that you cannot absorb great inner truths with the earthly mind, or with the intellect alone. You who read much may think you have garnered much knowledge – yet you may know so little. Lessons have to be learnt in your very being. The Master said, 'Whosoever shall not receive the kingdom of God as a little child, he shall not enter therein'. It really means this, dear ones: that you have to accept the daily experiences, and react to them always on a higher level, receiving and giving forth in the spirit of God, so far as you humanly can, and in accordance with your understanding of God. For it is

23

in those daily experiences and in the tests of every day that you learn to control the kingdom of yourself. You achieve mastery over the physical body, the mental body and the astral body, so that instead of your bodies being just a mass of jumbled colour and vibration, they become orderly, working in perfect rhythm and harmony, each responding to the spiritual plane of being to which it belongs.

Don't think you have to be a crank, but rather be human, and express yourself harmoniously. Enjoy life . . . be good, be God – God, who would have you enjoy the gifts and the fruits of the earth, and all the beauties of the earth. But also you have to cultivate that higher self which enables you to see the beauty lying behind the physical form of your brethren, of your brother animal, the plants, your companions the glorious mountains, the streams, and the wind in the trees, the beauty of the stars. Live harmoniously in this way and you will surely find the God that Jesus told you to love.

All these secrets Jesus completely possessed. He had passed through schools of training in many, many incarnations before he came to earth. He was not merely master of what you would call psychic law, but of the spiritual law, the law of God, the creative law. As your records in the gospels show, he was able to create and change physical form; he was able to bring people back to life from apparent death. What enabled such miracles to occur as, for instance, when Jesus, the beloved Master, walked on the water? The simple explanation we would give is this: that he was so at one with God the Father that as he walked he did not think of the water beneath his feet; he did not look down fearing he must sink in the water. With utter completeness of attention he thought only of God the Father. Can you catch a fleeting understanding, and glimpse the power which would so sustain the physical body that it could not sink? We say that by the very act of thinking of God Jesus was filled with the love and the light of God the Father and so his body became buoyant, no longer 'of the earth, earthy', but suffused with the light of God.

How did he control the elements when the disciples were terrified of drowning because of the storm at sea? When the boat was tossed by the wind and sea Jesus slept; your bible says that the disciples were sore afraid, and awakened him crying, 'Lord, save us: we perish'. Now remember that Jesus was Master – master of all the elements both without and also within the kingdom of his own being. Those devas and great ones of the angelic kingdom who control the powers of nature would feel the utter harmony, respond to the call of a being who had attained to that perfect mastery. And how had he attained? Through love, through the spirit of peace which dwelt in him. How can a man hope to control the elements when he does not know peace within himself? But the Master, having completely attained to the peace of God, had won the power of command over the elementals and the nature spirits. He controlled the elements – not of himself, not of his own mind and will, but by the power and love of the God within him. We assure you that to be a spiritual scientist, in however small a degree, man has to tread each step of the way by his daily life and aspirations; to tread the path of selflessness, of daily communion with the love of the Father–Mother God, and to set himself on one side. 'Thy will be done in earth, as it is being done in heaven.'

What of the changing of water into wine?* We only attempt to give you hints of the law underlying physical matter, but we could say that Jesus raised and changed the vibrations of the atoms of which the physical substance was composed. If the vibrations of the atoms in physical matter are changed, the atoms take on a different form. Matter in different forms vibrates at different rates. We want you to understand that for Jesus, working from the creative plane of spirit, it was possible by changing the rate of vibration of the

* On other occasions White Eagle has given a deep mystical interpretation of this miracle, as indeed of others. See *The Living Word of St John* (White Eagle Publishing Trust, 1979), pp.16–17.

26

atoms, to change the water into another substance
– as, in this instance, he changed it into wine.

It was always by the same method: not of his
own power, but by the Father which dwelt in
him . . . 'The Father that dwelleth in me, he
doeth the works . . . I and my Father are one.'
We would try to convey to you that Christ the
Son, the light of the Logos, completely illumined
the human personality of Jesus of Nazareth.

The Prodigal Son

EVEN THOUGH you may know nothing about esoteric teaching, your own intuition can help you
to understand so much of inner truth. It is not
necessary to be a student of any particular school,
so long as you are a student who learns through
human nature and human reactions, particularly
your own. We do not mean a study too particularly
of your own self, but rather a going forth and a
living and expressing of the Christ within in
actual life, allowing the Christ within to control
emotion and desire and the arrogant mind. The
hymn which we hear our brethren sing, 'Breathe
through the heats of our desire' . . . breathe the
breath of God . . . beautifully expresses what is
first needed to prepare the way for illumination.
As soon as man begins to encourage and listen to
that still small voice within, he begins to develop
spiritually, without great esoteric knowledge. It

is a natural process, through the drawing to himself of those vibrations of light which release powers within his soul which in turn enable it to bring through to his physical brain understanding of the life of the unseen. This growth of the light within eventually reveals the true life, and brings an expansion of consciousness and intelligence, enabling him to read the heavens and the earth . . . and to understand men's hearts. Even as the beloved Jesus the Christ read and understood the hearts of his brethren.

You can do much to help the growth of the light in men's hearts by endeavouring to think and act in a *real* way. What do we mean by a 'real way'? We speak of the reality of human kindness. We think of the great teachers, particularly the Master Jesus, and see in their teaching a wonderful understanding. We would on this occasion stress the human love of the Master Jesus. His life was the human life. What do children feel about Jesus? Spontaneously they love him, and love to hear of his miracles and parables. The children do not question, nor try to understand intellectually. They only know Jesus as a loving man, a kind and gentle spirit, and say their prayers to Jesus because they feel in their hearts that Jesus will understand.

Beloved brethren, Jesus *does* understand. God understands! Do you see what we mean? The child naturally and spontaneously loves that gracious and strong figure, Jesus. The Cosmic Christ manifested through Jesus, by reason, we suggest, of his simplicity and humility. He did not set himself up in high places, but walked the earth in simplicity, and made a friend of the sinner. His teaching stressed the point of the so-called sinner being beloved of his Father. He had no time for hypocrisy. You remember the woman whom the world had cast out? She came to Jesus, drawn to him by that spontaneous love which she felt in her heart for him. She knew that he would not reject her. Her intuition told her that here, in this one man, dwelt real love, true compassion. Real love: not a condescending love, but a love which would enfold her and give her friendship and peace, something to hold on to. And so she knelt at his feet and washed them with her tears, and anointed them with precious ointment. We speak of this incident purely on the outer plane, although there is an inner meaning, too: always Jesus' teaching was both for the outer forms of life, and for the inner planes.

We would like to take this opportunity of elucidating the story of the elder and younger brother in the parable of the prodigal son. Think of these two aspects. The younger brother did not know much about life, but he had certain gifts given to him by his father, and he made up his mind to enjoy these gifts – and he did. He lived to the full. He wasted his substance, so we are told, in riotous living. Caught up in the desires of the earthly life, he wasted his substance. We do not advocate that you all spend your substance in riotous living! But we would have you see another aspect of this story. The younger son went out into a far land, and lived on the outer plane, to the fullest extent. He was not sleepy and lethargic; whatever he did, he thoroughly enjoyed. You have heard us say, 'enjoy life; bless your food and enjoy it; enjoy all God's gifts and life's experience, but always praise your Father God for that which is given. Thank God, and enjoy his gifts'. Human experience can bring, in time, so much wisdom and true light.

The prodigal son, after dissipating all his substance, was brought to the lowest depths. Have you ever thought what jewel may be hidden in the man who is, as you would say, 'down to the dregs' – what jewel may be lying within that ugly casket? The son arose, for the light came into him, and he realised that he was working as a hireling for another master, not his father. Oh, how many work for another master, one who is harsh, maybe, and holds the soul in subjection! There came a time when the prodigal son realised this, and he rose up and went back to his father: 'Father, I have sinned' – the first step, the acknowledgment of his mistake – 'I am no more worthy to be called thy son: make me as one of thy hired servants'. Notice the humility, the utter love and expectancy; he knew he would not be turned away. His soul, his intuition, had told him that.

Now, what of the elder brother who had remained with his father throughout? There was no celebration for him, no rejoicing: 'Son, thou art ever with me', said his father; 'all that I have is thine'. The elder son had remained with his father, and had worked for him. But why? Was it because he spontaneously wanted nothing more than the privilege of service? It is possible for those who tread an occult path to live and work with the thought – maybe unconscious – that they are thereby making good karma: they may become absorbed in their own spiritual progress. The prodigal son did not think about himself or his karma. He went out and he lived, and he expressed his humanity, and when he found that life reduced him to nothing, he returned to his father bringing with him a rich harvest of experience, of karma – will you understand us if we even say, good karma? – through that human contact. He may have squandered his substance, but he was kindly, he gave freely, and did not think about his own soul.

Jesus spoke of the elder brother as self-righteous; so self-righteous that he was annoyed with his father for having received his own brother! One of the teachings of the inner schools is that the elder brother must always help the younger, and rejoice in his progress – rejoice when the younger is brought into the home of the Father. That was the elder brother's great test; and one which comes to us all. Do we work to build up good karma for ourselves, or are we living and giving life to all humanity, so that humanity shall reap the benefit? Live not to yourself, said the Master, so that you can squeeze through the gates of heaven. Forget yourself. What do we matter? We are nothing very much. But what does life matter; what does the whole of the human race matter? They are God's children.

Let us so live, not that we may scrape into heaven, but that through our expression of the light, we show forth Christ. We cannot aspire without helping our brother; we cannot act kindly, lovingly, generously, not only in a material sense but in our thoughts and attitude towards our brother man, without helping all. 'If I be lifted up from the earth' – the Christ within – 'I will draw all men unto me'. Whatever we have learnt – or think we have learnt – let us all live as the children of earth, the simple children . . . the younger sons, our brethren.

Reincarnation and Karma

ON THE occasion when this talk was given, White Eagle had been asked to give his interpretation of a familiar phrase from the bible. From this he turned to talk about the question of reincarnation and karma:

We were once asked to give our explanation of the words, 'visiting the iniquity of the fathers upon the children unto the third and fourth generation'.

In pondering these words from the Old Testament you must remember that as far as the earthly civilisation was concerned, the early Israelites were like children. Their life was cruder than that of humanity at the present time, and because of this many were much in the flesh, and living for the gratification of the lower self. Therefore law was necessary to check, to teach them to follow the God of heaven, not of the lower self. They had to learn discipline and self-control, and you notice that the appeal was made to the parental instinct. At a certain stage of evolution in the human civilisation you will find that the parental is the strongest instinct; therefore that instinct was being appealed to: you must not sin; you must not corrupt the body; if you do it means that the children created from your body will be afflicted with the disease which your self-indulgence has caused to be in your own bloodstream.

It is natural for the reason of man to rise up and rebel against the interpretation once put on these words – 'If God is a God of love, it seems completely unjust that innocent children should suffer for the sins of their fathers'. It is a little like a question about which we see many of our earthly brethren become disturbed. You witness outrages, persecution, suffering, and Providence vouchsafes no reason.

Why are some people born to enjoy a long life of health and achievement while others are born crippled, maimed, or as hopeless and helpless invalids? Why indeed are some favoured with, and others denied, the opportunities for which they long? Why are some children born into homes and circumstances of supreme harmony and happiness, with every cultural and material opportunity, while others find themselves inmates of homes of discord and misery? Is the soul entirely unresponsible, entirely innocent when it must endure such harshness and hardship? If so, how can one reconcile such a state of injustice with an all-wise, all-loving Father God? Life when viewed on the surface can give no answer. We must look deeper; and without an understanding of the law of reincarnation the suffering and inequalities, spiritual, mental, physical and material of our fellow-creatures cannot be harmonised with the statement 'God is love'.

Although many need no convincing of the truth of reincarnation, there are still some who find the whole idea very unpalatable. One who is wearied by his experience on earth, and who longs for the heavenly life, for the peace and beauty that he believes awaits him after death, naturally feels he will not want to come back after tasting the joys of heaven. Yet such a return to the prosaic is continually happening on earth. You may go to some beautiful play, or hear glorious music and are uplifted in your spirit; nevertheless next morning there awaits the office, or the kitchen. You come down to earth from heaven with a jolt. However lovely the concert was, or the play, however great your enjoyment, nevertheless you have had to come and get on with your work.

A rather similar state exists in the heaven world . . . as above, so below; as below, so above. Whilst the soul, the highest part of man, contacts those finer spheres of spirituality and truth, it is happy, and it absorbs the infinite wisdom. But the innermost self, the individuality, knows that it has work to do, not necessarily only to help humanity (although that is part of the great plan of incarnation), but also work to do upon his own soul.

To make this point clear, we would liken the soul of man to a temple in the heavens. No one incarnation is expressing the whole of that soul. The you which is manifesting on earth is only a part of that greater self. Your greater self is living in the spiritual spheres. From this greater self the still voice within the heart receives the directions which the soul needs. It is not possible for humanity to express or manifest the fullness of that higher self whilst in the physical body, any more than even the Master Jesus could fully express the greatness and glory of Christ. The higher self, being in contact with the spheres of truth, knows what material the temple needs for its building and completion. You know the biblical story of the building of the temple, and how the lily-work was left to the last? Or the reference to the temple not built with hands, but eternal in the heavens? You do not mind coming back, you know you have work to do, that your temple is not finished; therefore you return to earth with a purpose, and by contributing your very finest work, by giving love and understanding and companionship to your brother man, you perhaps complete the lily-work. You do not question; you know there is a purpose and a necessity for your return.

No soul is forced back into incarnation. A soul comes back directed by the higher self . . . call it God if you like, but the intuition sends that soul back into incarnation. Before a child is born, the higher aspect of that soul is shown the possibilities which lie before it. If you incarnate into this family, certain things are likely to happen, but these experiences will, used wisely, bring to you a certain strength of the soul, a certain quality of consciousness which you need. Bear this in mind: the soul comes back of its own desire in order to gain experience and to develop certain qualities of God-consciousness. It may even be that the soul sees that by incarnation in a certain family it will be liable to a certain problem of health, because the tendency towards that disease or disability will be transmitted. The soul will be told: 'You can enter into that life, tackle that problem, and see if you can rise above it; it is not necessary for you to suffer if you can bring into operation the law of love'.

We often talk of the transmutation of karma. Whilst the soul takes on these earth conditions, if it does not respond to the God-urge within, it will possibly succumb, and suffer; but *through* such suffering it will eventually learn, and pass to freedom. It will be following the usual course of the law of karma. But should the soul take the other way, opening its consciousness to the true God life and bringing it into operation, it makes a jump, so to speak. It is possible for the inflow of divine life from the higher self, or temple in the heavens, to shine so strongly in that physical body, that all the weakness bequeathed by so-called heredity passes away. This is one instance of what we mean by the transmutation of karma. Most people take the ordinary way, and succumb to suffering. But *that is not the only way*; there is the other way, the higher path. We try to show you through this example how the light of the spirit can transmute the conditions of a man's life.

Our beloved Master Jesus spoke these words: 'Thou shalt love the Lord thy God with all thy heart, and with all thy soul, and with all thy mind, and with all thy strength . . . Thou shalt love thy neighbour as thyself'. By this he came to show, to teach, the *new* law. With the advent of Christ, the Christ light which shone through the human personality of Jesus, came a new revelation, to help humanity to speed up its evolution – a vital necessity at certain periods. Jesus came to bring new light on the old law: by divine love in the heart, man could rule the kingdom of himself, and bring upon earth the kingdom of heaven.

The purpose of incarnation is that the soul of man may be perfected. Man made perfect through physical experience. Do not think that reincarnation means retrogression. Reincarnation is progress, not the reverse: reincarnation means that failure and death are not the end of a man; that the soul, whatever its shortcomings, is given an opportunity of re-living its life in matter, not once or twice, but possibly many times; and that with each rebirth it is presented with fresh opportunities to develop within itself a divine and selfless love – which is but another term for the Christ within. Man is fundamentally the child, the son or daughter of our Father–Mother God. Being made in God's image man has been endowed with Godlike potentialities. Only through the development of these gifts to the fullest extent is man able to enjoy the fruits of his spiritual heritage, and to know unalloyed happiness 'such as this world can neither give nor take away'.

When your inner vision is opened, and you see God, even if only the Godlike radiating through another personality, you at least are called upon to admire, to respect, to revere. But if your vision is still more opened, and you enter heaven and catch a picture of the perfect Son of God, he who is the Lord of this earth, you want only one thing: to get nearer, to be able to talk to that radiant being, to seek his companionship. It is only natural. Then your guardian angel will say to you, 'You admire, you revere that beautiful soul; you would like to draw nearer to this great brother, to become more like him?' And you reply, 'Above all things!' Then comes the answer: 'Then you shall. But you must tread your ordained path; you must go back again to the earth, and work on the material of your own temple. You must live your life with his image always before you. When you become as he, you will have the power to serve your fellow men, as he served'. Would a soul refuse, if the truth were thus presented?

Let us think in terms not of self alone, but in

terms of the good of all humanity, and let our life be a contribution to the whole. Let us give, so that we respond to the wisdom of the greater self, so that we climb away from the 'sins of the fathers' into freedom. With God all things are possible, and all may be healed, even as Christ himself continually demonstrated. Through his power, and through the response in the soul of the one whom he touched, the karma was transmuted, the soul illumined with the divine fire of Christ.

III

Jesus' Sayings and Parables

In these interpretations of various sayings and parables of Jesus, White Eagle shows how these beautiful utterances of Jesus not only refer to the outer life, but also reveal a path of inner unfoldment.

The Kingdom of Heaven is within You

We want to say something to you about true religion. True religion is not tied to any creed or dogma, it is not merely some form of belief. *Religion is the growing consciousness of God in man's own being.* When man becomes awakened to the light of God, then the Christ within him, the Son of God within him, starts to grow; and this growing God-consciousness is his strength and stay, his comfort and his guide. This is true religion, and it is what all humanity is searching for.

Today, western man has to a large extent foregone organised religion, but he is still seeking for God in many ways; and he will not get very far until he learns that the God he seeks is in himself. He can learn about this vital truth only through the love which he can feel for others,

41

and compassion for the sufferings, the inharmony and pain which shadow his brother's life. When he recognises these he starts to think what he can do to alleviate this suffering, and then the first glimmerings of religion dawn in man's heart. Thereafter he will desire to change his own life, wanting to live in accordance with his new inner feeling – a feeling of love, love for God and for all life, growing slowly in his heart. As this feeling of concern and love for his brother grows, it enfolds more than human life; it expands into other worlds, into the animal, the natural kingdoms; then beyond all physical form into the etheric and so into the mental kingdom and to the celestial kingdom. The consciousness of God, which once started as a tiny spark, grows and expands until finally that soul embraces all life, both physical and spiritual; there is no limitation to his consciousness of God. Then this man can no longer harm his brother by thought or word or deed. He becomes gentle in his ways, meek but never weak. Remember the example of Jesus: not only his gentle nature, his meekness, but also his resolute strength, his moral courage – and his unfailing compassion for those who sinned and suffered.

Man, in his search for religion, must look beyond the shells of orthodoxy, creed and dogma, for the indwelling spirit in his brother man. True religion in a man gives him complete conviction beyond shadow of doubt, that he cannot die and that those whom he loves can never die. He needs no proof of continuing life after death. He already knows, because the light within him reveals higher worlds of a purer ether into which the spirit passes.

Treasure in Heaven

You are living an outer life in a physical world. But side by side with this outer life there is an inner life. This inner life is a world of thought; and thought promotes action. Now, as a man thinks, so he becomes – he is creating his inner world. From that inner world come his speech and action. When the time comes for the spirit finally to leave the body, it goes into what may be described as an inner world, which has been created by thought. Thought is the impetus, is the seed of action. So obviously, if you look for a heaven world that is beautiful and peaceful, you must strive to attain that world of beauty and peace within yourself, within your soul, in your thoughts; because this is the world that one day awaits you.

There is a story of a woman of high degree who when she died expected to have all her earthly grandeur renewed in the spirit world. When she found herself very poor, she asked her guide why she lacked the splendour and courtesy to which she had formerly been accustomed, and her guide explained to her that she had not given them sufficient material to build a beautiful home, for her home was created out of the material which she herself supplied through her life on earth.

Then there was the story of the poor cobbler who devoted much of his time to mending very poor children's boots and shoes. He worked conscientiously with love in his heart and mind, thinking of the little feet that needed protection. He put his very best work into all his boot-mending. He was very poor but had a great love for and trust in God; and when he passed over he was met by a shining spirit who conducted him to his home, which was beautiful but simple, with lovely gardens and wonderful scenery. He knew that he had come to heaven.

In the spirit life, when the soul passes onward, everything depends on the thought-life. If the thoughts are good, the speech and the actions will be good. In this way the soul creates beauty for itself and others to enjoy. Everything begins with thought, so it is essential that thoughts are pure, humble, and harmonious, and that such thoughts are sent out to create harmony in life. In your physical life, even if you are living in difficult conditions, if you can remain harmonious within yourself, you are creating harmony. These harmonious thoughts will spread and you will be surprised at what can and will be done on earth by the infiltration of this spiritual light and brotherhood.

The Wedding Garment

There are in man spheres of consciousness of life far removed from what he knows on the physical plane, and these can be reached by all who will create within themselves the necessary conditions. It is not necessary for you to pass from the earth plane before entering into the spheres of beauty. Indeed, you are not likely to find those planes of heavenly bliss unless you have developed the particular vehicle in your earthly life which will enable you to dwell in that heaven world. Man is wont to say: 'Why bother about these spheres of spiritual life whilst dwelling on earth? There will be plenty of time for these when I have passed away from earth'.

On earth, if you desire to go to a particular function, you wear a dress suitable for the occasion, and if you do not clothe yourself rightly, you are unable to enter the function. How can man expect to participate in the joys of the heavenly life if he has no clothing, no aura, no senses developed which will enable him to contact such spheres of life? Meditation alone will not give you the requisite clothing, or vehicle, but simply *being* love in all your relationships will clothe you in raiment suitable for you to meet the king.

(In this teaching, White Eagle throws further light on the subject of karma.)

Why is it that some people apparently have many opportunities and others few or none? Why is it that some souls endure much sorrow and others seem to sing through life? There is an answer to be found to all these questions in the truth, the law, of reincarnation and of karma. If you lack opportunity it is for a very good reason. The opportunities which now seem to be withheld will most certainly be given in a future life. If your eyes were open and you could see the whole circle of your many lives you would perhaps see that some time in the past you had neglected your opportunities. You will also see that in the future you will have your chance again.

From this you will understand how important it is to be on the alert so that we do not miss the opportunity when it comes, for opportunities may pass. How often men have said, 'Oh, if only I had my chance over again, I would be so different. If only I could go to school again I would not waste my time!'

Well, you either progress steadily and surely along the path of evolution; or you delay, you can digress. We are reminded of the parable of the wise and the foolish virgins. The wise kept their lamps filled with oil. What was that oil? It was the wisdom of the spirit. Their lamps were filled with spiritual wisdom, the wick kept well trimmed so that the flame burned clearly. The foolish did not bother. Their lamps were empty at the time when they were wanted, their wicks untrimmed. They went away weeping – they returned from whence they came. If *our* lamps be empty we shall return from whence we came to face the same lesson in another life. We had our opportunity once; but when we went forth to meet our Lord and Master we were not ready.

We of the spirit work very closely with you all. It is our mission. We have passed through all the experiences of earth life which are now yours and we understand your difficulties. We suffer with you; we rejoice with you. Therefore, we know that it behoves all who would be wise to fill their lamps with spiritual wisdom, so that when they go to meet the Master they will be prepared. How disappointing to be waiting; and just as the Master draws near, to have to return!

This is a parable of reincarnation. Of course, it has many other explanations. Shall we say that there are seven explanations or interpretations of this and other parables; they can be interpreted on seven different planes of consciousness? We have given you one interpretation only.

To answer another question which may arise, we suggest that you think of the soul as a great star, a jewel which has many facets. The life or the soul of man is like this jewel; and each facet is an earth life. So when the soul reincarnates it is not necessarily the same aspect of that soul which comes down again to earth. Another facet, it may be, sends forth a stream of life which penetrates physical matter. The child is born again on earth. While that soul is descending to earth life it is being clothed, made ready for its new experiences. On earth it gains further experiences. The soul actually asks before it comes that it may have difficulties to overcome, and opportunities to wipe out mistakes made in a former journey to earth. When it leaves the earth it remains for a short time on the astral plane, then passes through the mental planes into the celestial world and finds its true home again, being reunited to the greater self in the heavens. It takes back with it as a harvest the experiences it has gained – we pray, a wealth of experience.

We have endeavoured to be simple in dealing with this profound subject. This is our parting word; whatever experience is yours on earth *use* it. Do not be neglectful. Take back with you wisdom and love; but, of course, wisdom is love – both are inseparable. One who is all love is all wisdom. One who is all wisdom is all love. We do not understand wisdom divorced from love nor love divorced from wisdom. Above all, make use of every day you live. Patiently and confidently do your best on the material plane, whether you work in workshop, office, factory, church or school. Make your home beautiful and serve the comfort of your fellows in that home. Whatever your hand finds to do, do it from your very heart, because you are a child of God, and he has given you the gift of mind, of heart, of hands to labour, and of kindly speech. These are your tools, with which to work on earth.

My brethren, let us be true to the spirit, let us be sounded again and again, and each time ring true. If we are put through the fires of suffering, let us be thankful, because we are being purified and the metal so tested that only pure gold will remain. This is the meaning of the phrase 'the turning of base metal into gold'. The gold of the spirit remains sound after the base metal of the lower nature has been extracted.

The Parable of the Talents

We would like to consider with you the story of the talents. You will remember that those who had the greatest blessing in return had first learnt how to make the best use of their blessing. The one who had received only a small blessing of one talent of silver failed to value even that. People still puzzle over this parable. We can only say that it is important for any man who has received knowledge of the spiritual life to make use of that knowledge, and not to bury it. This is especially so at this present time. People fail to live by truth which has been revealed to them. By so doing they bury the light of truth. My children, you have been given a grave trust; your responsibility is to make use of the gift of knowledge which has been given you, because if you do not – if you cover up your talent, and bury it – in future days you may find that you have lost your talent, which means that in some future life you will have lost your spiritual awareness.

Try not to accept such gifts, my children, without due thankfulness. Do not take things for granted. Realise that the smallest faculty, whatever it may be, is entrusted to you as a talent to be used for the blessing of your brother man. Therefore by constant aspiration make yourself a clear channel for the pouring through of the divine light of the Sun; for as mother earth receives the sunlight which stimulates and causes the seed to grow, so you, each in your degree, are that mother earth. When God has given man the seed, no matter whether it be a seed to plant, or a spiritual seed – which means some attainment of the soul – remember that it is for spiritual sowing. Your spiritual seeds are given to you, not to keep to yourself, but to sow again in life, so that others may benefit from your sowing.

The soul of man can be likened to the earth,

the mother; and the Sun, the spirit, the Christ light, is the seed planted in the heart of every man, woman and child. The purpose of man's life is to bring forth this child, the Christ child, that the earth may be peopled with happiness. God does not condemn mankind to sorrow, to a life of wretchedness. God has given life to his sons and daughters that they may enjoy greater glories. It is therefore our work – yours on earth, ours in spirit – to help in the harvesting, the bringing forth of the fruits of the spiritual life upon earth.

In Revelation there is a passage which tells of the twenty-four elders around the throne of God, casting their crowns before him. The twenty-four elders can symbolise the souls who have achieved, who have attained, divine illumination or spiritual realisation. They are crowned with the golden crown of perfect life. When you are filled with the power of the spirit even as – to an infinitely greater degree – the elders around the throne were filled with the divine light, there is no other way for you than to give back your harvest. The man who becomes spiritually illumined, who has found the joy of spiritual inspiration and love, must give and give and give to his fellow man. He cannot do otherwise; he must give back to God that which is God's, even as the twenty-four elders around the throne cast down their crowns before him. When the soul has attained fullness of knowledge, of under-standing, it can but give back again that which it has received, so loving has it become.

Good and Evil: and the Money-Changers in the Temple

We ask you to try to think of so-called evil in terms of undeveloped goodness, undeveloped godliness. To us in spirit, darkness is really unconsciousness, the unconsciousness of physical matter to God. Yet brethren, all aspects of life are contained within the Creator. If you believe that God is all-powerful, all-wise and all-loving, that God contains everything, God cannot rule here and what you call the devil rule over there. God is the whole; God holds all within his grasp, all is within his divine Intelligence.

You ask us if it is right to attack this or that state of apparent evil which you see in the world. Our answer, brethren, is that when you go into a darkened room, if you are wise you carry a light. This is what we in spirit would do to remove evil: we would take a light. When there is light, no darkness remains. The true way to deal with evils is to help the world towards a state of spiritual knowledge and wisdom; otherwise you are often only scratching the soil. Of course it is helpful and right to remove and reform bad physical conditions, bad ways of living. This is all part of a process of evolution and growth, for it is part of man's work to create beauty. Therefore you will naturally do all you can to bring about a state of godliness, of purity and happiness on earth. But you have to prepare the way by being true and balanced in your thought of the Great White Spirit, knowing in your inmost soul that God is wholly wise and wholly beneficient; knowing that whatever experiences God's children have to go through, these experiences come in order to give an expansion of vision, an expansion of spiritual life within.

You have the words of Jesus, 'Resist ye not evil'; and the initiate Paul said, 'Overcome evil with good'. In other words, let your light – the true light of God – shine upon darkness, and the darkness dissolves. You do not create antagonism. You quietly pursue the path of the Christ spirit by living the Christ life, expressing the light and love of the Sun in any adverse condition. In this way you are overcoming darkness with light.

It is claimed that the Master Jesus seems to have condemned evil-doers. He is said to have taken a whip to drive the money-changers from the temple, saying 'It is written, My house shall be called a house of prayer, but you have made it a den of thieves!' Now, what did the Master really mean by this? As we interpret this story, the temple is man's own being, his own nature. You are the temple; and within you dwells the spirit of God; but if you become absorbed in the lower nature that is greedy and brutal and full of fear, if you submit to such elements you will fill your temple with thieves and robbers. Then the Christ or the Master within you will rise up and say, 'Be gone! this is the house of God!' The story then applies primarily to man's own being.

It appears that the Master on other occasions expressed indignation – righteous indignation it is called – at evil doers. We would again see this first as an illustration of the Christ spirit, the Master of man's mind. It is natural that the Master rises up and claims his own conditions. When Christ claims his own status he must of necessity be casting out from the temple that which is disturbing the beauty of the God-state that should rule in the temple. Christ is the light which beautifies and makes strong every human spirit.

Ask, Seek, Knock

You people on earth do not really understand how the spirit brethren work with you. It is not good that we should relieve you of your karma, indeed we cannot; but we are permitted to help you, to give you opportunities to transmute your own karma. We are permitted to help you with much love, even as a mother is permitted to help her children. So the brethren in the world of spirit are enabled to come back and help you.

You must do the best you can for yourselves without anxiety; then you must have confidence in the power of the light to take charge, to help you. The Master once said, 'Oh ye of little faith!' 'According to your faith be it unto you.' This means first, faith in the eternal love; then faith in your own elder brethren. Do the elder brethren in a family refuse to come to the aid of their younger brethren? How much more then do the elder brethren of the spirit family come to the aid of their brethren in the flesh.

'Ask and ye shall receive; seek and ye shall find the truth; knock and the door of heaven shall be opened unto you.' You forget the spirit behind these words. Seek truth in all sincerity; seek it in the quiet chambers of your own heart. Seek and ye shall find that contact with the eternal love, the eternal power. Ask of that love and that power. Ask and the supply will be unfailing – the spiritual supply, the supply of spiritual power which will flow through you and your life, enabling you to forget yourself and to rise in service to your fellow men. Then knock; knock on the door of initiation, the temple door, the door of heaven. Knocking on the door means action. Act according to the law; so through your action you knock on the door of heaven, which is also the door of initiation. Then the bandage falls from your eyes and you are bidden to enter the temple unblindfolded; and you see eternal truth.

We want to show you the wonderful love of God and the wonderful provision God has made for you. For you have been given within your heart the seed-atom of the Christ spirit. You have it in *yourself* to create, to bring about your own redemption in your own conditions, in your own surroundings, by your right thought towards life, towards other people, and your thoughts about yourself. This is why we say that only you can open the door which leads to a higher state of consciousness for you.

We stress again that God has placed within every being a saviour – although man so often will not listen to the promptings of his saviour, but gives way to what you call the devil. There is a certain degree of truth in this old doctrine. Is it not man's lower self which is the real evil or devil in him? Evil means the devil, and the devil is the tempter, but it is not wholly bad, because man is also given opportunity to resist, to rise above, to overcome evil. Resistance really means the rising up of the noble Christ-man in him so that evil is overcome.

The story of the temptations in the wilderness tells of this, when Jesus said: 'Get thee behind me, Satan'. The children of earth unfortunately do not recognise that the weakness of human nature is a temptation. They excuse themselves and say: 'Oh, we are only human. What else can you expect?' Even as we speak to you and use your earthly language, confusion can creep in. To put it very plainly once again; man's lower nature is both his tempter and his devil. To overcome temptation strengthens the spirit of Christ within. You must be stern with yourself; but you must also see that other people are struggling (even as you continually struggle) to find that Christ help. When you once realise this, it robs you of all desire to condemn others. Did not Jesus say: 'Judge not, that ye be not judged'? – and when you come to the spirit life you will realise that while you are your own judge, yet you cannot judge another.

So, you see, everything that man needs for his salvation, for his peace of mind and happiness, lies within himself. God gives to all his children power to save themselves. Perhaps you now see the meaning of the phrase 'salvation of the world by Christ'. Salvation by the Christ in you. 'I came', he said, 'that you might have eternal life.'

Judge Not

It is so easy to judge the actions of others, but, dear children, do try to refrain from judgment, for as you condemn others, so you condemn yourself. Strive to be tolerant and to give from your heart the gentle spirit of the master soul.

Jesus the Christ is one such master soul, man made perfect, and this highly evolved and perfected soul incarnated in order to reveal to individual man what he could himself attain to if he followed the simple, gentle way of the Christ.

Forgive, my children, forgive! Whatever is in your heart, however hard you may feel towards any soul, possibly with justification according to material standards, pray to forgive as Jesus taught in his simple prayer: 'Forgive us our trespasses, as we forgive those who trespass against us'. Do you not realise that in forgiving others, you are releasing yourselves? As soon as you feel forgiveness in your own heart, you release yourself from the bondage of your karma. But so long as you sit in harsh judgment over your fellows, whether they be individual people or nations; so long as you continue to condemn, refusing to forgive, you bring that same judgment upon yourself, for life is ruled by spiritual law.

The Rich Young Man

Jesus said to the man who had asked him what he should do to gain eternal life: 'Sell all that thou hast, and distribute unto the poor'. 'And when he heard this, he was very sorrowful: for he was very rich.' This is usually interpreted to mean material riches, but the Master did not specify what kind. 'Sell all that thou hast, and distribute unto the poor.' In these words the very heart of the spiritual life is being touched, the motive behind the spiritual search and spiritual development. 'Sell all that thou hast!' – which means that man must be ready to surrender all that he most truly prizes; he must not clasp his possessions to himself, whether they be material or of a more subtle nature (and often it is on the higher plane of consciousness that the temptation is most subtle). All pride of possession must go, whether the possessions be worldly goods, mental attainments, or spiritual jewels.

The Revelation of St John describes the elders casting down their crowns before the throne of God . . . or 'selling all they possessed'. For the word 'elders' we should read 'initiates' or 'masters', those who have attained. They 'cast their crowns before the throne of God', knowing that man can hold nothing to himself. All he gains, all he learns, all he attains by striving through many lives he must surrender. Not of himself has he achieved, but by the spirit within, God in him. Is it not then fitting he surrenders all that he has and is to God?

Pride of possession forms a temptation which all face in varied forms, but all have in the end to arrive at that point of spiritual growth where they know that they possess nothing. Of ourselves we are nothing, we possess nothing; for all gifts, all attainments, come from God and belong to

God. We live and move and have our being only in the consciousness of our Father–Mother God. All that we think we possess, all that we think we have, can be taken away at a stroke, so that we are bereft of all – all, that is, except consciousness of the complete fullness and richness and wealth of God's life. So whilst man actually possesses nothing, and must be brought to that realisation, yet he has it within his consciousness to be a part of the whole, and in this realisation he is wealthy beyond the dreams of earthly wealth. In coming into the realisation of true wealth man becomes part of the great universal power, which is his to use, not for himself, but for the good of the whole.

We have tried to make it clear that the object behind the quest for spiritual learning, growth and attainment must be this God-consciousness, this surrender, this selling all thou hast or this casting down the crown of glory before the throne of God. Man cannot hold to himself; it is against spiritual law.

Two Commandments

We would again emphasise the beauty and simplicity expressed in the work and life of Jesus. He told you plainly the two commandments upon which hangs all the law. Man must first love God. Now immediately man's spirit goes forth in adoration to God, his heart subtly contacts the rest of all creation, and particularly human creation. He realises in a flash his at-one-ment with God. He knows that if God is in himself, God is also in his brother man. If man finds God in the holy of holies within his own soul, he knows without being preached at that his fellow man has been created in the same way as himself, and shares in the same holy light. If it is una-wakened, it is still there, waiting. He knows that his Master once said: 'Thou shalt love thy neigh-bour as thyself'; and that by giving out love to his neighbour he is helping him not only to deal with the practical problems of daily life, but also to awaken to the eternal God-consciousness within his neighbour. Jesus said: 'Love one another'. Just this! Yet some will say: 'This is only sen-timent, you want to get beyond sentiment!' But you cannot comprehend spiritual glory without love, because there is no glory visible for the soul who is loveless. However humble the soul that loves, it can enter into God.

'Thou shalt love thy neighbour as thyself.' Love of oneself is important, but this does not mean selfishness; it means kindliness to yourself because you are God's child. Do not give yourself more attention than you need, but take care of yourself and do not continually slay the God within you. Give opportunities in your daily life for the Christ within to manifest itself. This is what we mean by loving yourself, and this is what Christ meant by 'Thou shalt love thy neighbour as thyself'. Love peace of mind, love doing the right thing, love living according to divine law, which is the law of love, of purity.

Love thy neighbour and love thyself. Do good to your own soul not by thinking unduly about yourself but abiding by wise laws of right living, right eating, right thinking. Create as far as you can pure and right conditions in your home and surroundings, in your relationships. Try to understand the trials and the difficulties in another person's life which may make them act hurtfully. Turn away wrath by gentleness and love, remembering that as you feel hurt and irritated, so may your companion feel too. Until you can dispassionately feel with the feeling of your companion, you will not understand the life of a master soul.

The master soul is the gentle soul, the wise, loving and compassionate soul, patient in adversity, who never loses faith in God and his ministering angels.

This, my friends, is the meaning of at-one-ment. You see how it comes right into your everyday human relationships. You cannot do it all at once, we know: but, beloved friends, make a good try! and as you raise yourselves, you will raise all men.

IV

The Great Healer

As we have told you, Jesus was known as the great master-healer and teacher by many races of people throughout the ages. We ourselves knew and loved the Master Jesus a long, long time ago when we were living and serving in a temple on a continent now lost. We knew Jesus and we loved him; later, after other incarnations, we came into contact with him again when he came to our people from over the seas; he came with his healing touch, the gentle healer. He healed the sick body, and he healed the troubled mind. He brought light and peace, and our people loved him and thronged about him, and they never forgot him.

Jesus is not only the great soul, the great Master through whom Christ shines. He would have us tell you he is also your gentle brother. We of the brotherhood in spirit would tell you that you must regard Jesus as a close, beloved friend. In our age-old religion, we were taught when we were very young to meet this healer, this pure and perfect white brother. And he can come to you when you visualise him as we have

63

described him. Talk to him, open your heart. Have no fear, just confide in your heart in your gentle white brother, Jesus, who will come very close to you, closer than breathing. He says, 'Remember my words – except you become as a little child, you cannot enter the state of heaven or peace or happiness'. Imagine Jesus is by your side, talk to him; if your heart is troubled, if you are anxious about a patient for healing or a loved one, just call on Jesus. And do you know what he will say to you? We think he will say, 'My child, we are one with the heavenly Father. We three are one . . . we three are one'. And you will create such a vital power that the one you would protect or heal will be clothed in the whole armour of God.

If you are faced with a problem, if your heart is full of fear and anxiety for yourself or a loved one, take your burden to the Great Healer, talk to the Great Healer, listen . . . and you will be comforted, you will be given strength, and you will know that your loved one is being cared for by a greater love and a stronger power than your own. Always resign your problems to the Great Healer.

Attunement to the Healing Power

THE REMAINDER of this chapter concentrates not so much on the healing miracles as recorded in the bible, but on attunement to the healing power within, which can flow into human life. White Eagle describes not only the spirit of healing, but a healing science.

A Vision of Jesus the Healer

Beloved children, we would bring to you a message, a truth about the power of love. You hear so much said about love, that the spoken word seems to lose its power, but we would bring to your hearts the emotion of love, the feeling of love. Do stop thinking about your physical cares and your material anxieties and concentrate upon the sweet, gentle emotion of love. We know that if you will train yourselves to think in terms of love every moment of life, you will find that unconsciously a beautiful healing will take place.

There are many methods of healing but there is only one true source from which healing power flows. This is the foundation of life, of love. Now the Master Jesus is the head of the healing ray. It is his special work to help humanity to get that contact with the source of life. It is a mystical truth that you are within his presence whenever you humbly and truly aspire to the source of all healing.

We would that we could convey to you the gentle simplicity of his figure, of his personality. He is living in the light of his Father–Mother God. He sees, he knows only the light, and this is what we must all endeavour to do. Although he is at one with the Father, he does not come with great pomp and ceremony. He just comes as a simple brother, a son of God, and he comes to each one of you according to your need. It is just a touch upon your shoulder or upon your hand or your brow; but it is in the silence and the stillness that he comes . . .

Oh the figure, human, perfected by the inflowing light of Christ the Son! And when we learn to love and recognise that simple, gentle, tender form then we open the gateway to the greater light, the glorious Christ light. We see it shining through the Master Jesus and we feel it entering our own being, we feel it release that source of divine almighty power which is within our innermost being.

O Lord, beloved Master, thou wilt touch the sick and ease all pain. Thou wilt give hope and inner peace to the weary and thou wilt give comfort to the sad and the lonely. Thou wilt build a bridge between hearts and between states of life so that there will be no separation but all will meet in the heart of Christ and thus will they be healed. Amen.

The Bread of Life

Beloved children, we would like to draw your attention to the words of Jesus the Christ, 'I am the bread of life'. You become so familiar with

66

the scriptures that you do not take time to ponder the meaning of the words, and we would ask you to think about this teaching of Jesus, 'I am the bread of life'.

When we come back to the earth-consciousness we want to bring you food. We desire to give you the food for which you are hungering (although you may not know that you are hungering). We see our earthly brethren with bodies that are imperfect or diseased. So often, in some form or another, your bodies are out of harmony, and if you could but realise it the true healing that you need is the bread of life. It is the spirit of Christ, which is the light. When the body is sick it is in some way lacking the light. All disease will in due time be traced to this lack. It is true that the majority of humanity may suffer from ill-health but you can trace all disease and all sickness to this perhaps unconscious disharmony in the soul; to a hold-up in the inflow of the light – the light which is the bread of life.

You perhaps wonder how this can apply to you individually. So many diseases are due to the psychic centres, or the chakras as the eastern brethren call them, not functioning harmoniously; so that the glands beneath them do not function as they should, and because this is so the body manifests some symptom. According to the symptoms your medical science gives a name to the disorder. You have many, many names to describe disorders of the physical body. This is very helpful in the present state of spiritual development or evolution, but when man understands his whole being, when he understands the working of his higher bodies so that they are functioning harmoniously, then the physical body will lose this diseased state.

Of course it is a very wide subject, but we would again draw your attention to those words, 'I am the bread of life'. The I AM is the light of the Christ spirit in you, which also means that within you lies a reservoir of light. It can be very covered up, so that it is hardly visible, but you as patients and as healers can quietly lay aside all mental conflict and turn within to that place of light, that well of intuition and spiritual sensitivity; and you can become aware of the invisible company of healers, and the power which they bring, helping you to draw upon your own inner reservoir of light; and then you will know that you have been given the bread of life.

'I am the bread of life', said Christ, and the Christ is within your heart. The bread of life reposes in the heart chakra, but you must endeavour to enter the inner sanctuary and attune yourself to that power.

*

You must allow the power within you to come into operation. In this way you are opening

yourself to the divine inflow. Do not be anxious.
Just surrender yourself to the all-loving Father–
Mother God, for all is love and none of you need
fear life – either life here or the life in spirit.
There is nothing to fear at all.

Let Go

We see our beloved children on earth walking
the disciplinary road of this life on earth – and
we see how in their ignorance they make mistakes,
bringing upon themselves suffering and pain
and fears and anxieties. We understand from
our own personal experience how you come to
suffer the ills of the flesh. But we would remind
you that all these ills come to help the soul to
understand, to learn the wisdom of the gods.
Nothing is ever wasted; but you must seek to
benefit through the experiences of the physical
life, because through these things, if you take
your karma rightly, you will find for yourselves
that karma is the opportunity given to each soul
to learn wisdom, to learn of the wondrous love
of God, of the Creator.

We suggest that one of the very first things
that you must learn to do when you have little
ailments in the physical body is to let them go.
Do not cling to them. The tendency in human
life is to hold fast to pain and disability, and
many people go so far as to think that their pain
and suffering is sent to them by God. My children,

God does not send your pain and your suffering to you, but the law of God says that inharmony in the soul sometimes has to work out through the physical body, and it is in this way that the true person, the soul, gains a deeper consciousness of the power of God which lies within its own being. All life's experiences have one object, and this is gradually to purify, to eliminate darkness, to bring light into the whole being. We would say it is to raise the mortal to the immortal.

We speak of a more profound truth than you realise. To raise the whole being from mortality to immortality means to raise it above the conflicting forces of the earth, above the bondage of matter, to raise it into those heights of spiritual glory which the saints and the illumined ones have been able to enjoy even whilst living in a physical body. Now, my dear ones, we do not expect you to do this all at once, but we want to explain to you that within you is the God-power, and that you are first and foremost children of God. Within you is the Sun, the light, the creative power, and it is the development of your soul, your spirit, which is the purpose of your life, and which will make you perfectly whole.

The Lord's Prayer as a Healing Affirmation

The white light has the power to heal the dark mental material conditions which oppress humanity. You draw to yourself the conditions that you think about. If you dwell on thoughts of sickness or limitation or poverty or fear, then you are setting up a vibration which is attracting those very conditions, or creating that which you fear. Train yourselves instead to set up a vibration of love, light, hope, confidence, peace, knowing that God your Father is all-wise and all-loving and that his will for you is that you should create about you the kingdom of heaven. The Master Jesus taught you that, for he said, 'When you pray, pray *Our Father which art in heaven*'. Our Father which art in a state of happiness and harmony, 'hallowed be thy name'. God, good, may the people on earth revere and hallow the name of all that is good. 'Thy kingdom come. Thy will be done in earth.' Thy will be done in the flesh and on earth, as thy will is done in a state of happiness which is heaven.

True prayer sets up a vibration in your soul which goes right to the source of supply. It must be true, sincere prayer, and there must be complete surrender of the soul to God's will. 'Thy will be done *in* earth': thy will be done in my physical body. God's will is good, and his will is that your body should be well, should be healthy, holy and able to enjoy all the good things, the spiritual things, the harmonious and beautiful things of life. The will of God for all his creation is that they may attain perfection and an

71

expansion of the little self into the great self, the Christ self. 'Give us this day our daily bread' – the bread which also can nourish the body of Christ within each man. Give us each day thy bread, thy sustenance that the Christ in man may be sustained and nourished. Thou wilt give us our dily bread and food on all planes of being.

'Forgive us our trespasses as we forgive . . .': the law of karma, for as you forgive so you are forgiven. 'Lead us not into temptation, but deliver us from evil.' This statement, my children, means that as you seek to be led into the ways of light and love you will not be overwhelmed with the sorrows of darkness. You are asking to be led into the spheres of light. 'For thine is the kingdom.' The kingdom is really the consciousness of God our Father. Thine is the kingdom of our souls, of our true nature; thine is the kingdom and in that kingdom is the power over all limitation. 'Thine is the kingdom, the power and the glory.' When you enter into that light you feel that your whole being is brought into harmony by the divine power and the glory which flows from the true, heavenly state of life. When you have learnt to dwell in the light of the Father–Mother God you will live in this consciousness even though you are using a physical body. Once you have touched the glory of the God-life you know that your true being is in this eternal light.

Seeking Spiritual Healing

The very first thing required for spiritual healing is for the patient and the healer to leave aside all the disturbances of the physical and material life; to withdraw from them, and seek the innermost sanctuary where all is peace. Now, my brethren, when we learn to think in terms of true peace, we relax, and we know within us that all is well. There are inconveniences and disturbances on the earth plane which maybe you think we do not have in the spirit life. We do not have them in the same way, it is true, but you who are still living in the body have to learn to relax the nervous system and to seek the inner tranquillity. When you are able to do this truly, you will become aware of a glow of power. There is a centre which is situated in the vicinity of the heart, right in the centre of the breast, and in perfect health it is radiating a life-force which can be seen by those who are clairvoyant as a soft pink colour. When you are attuned, lovingly, to the all-enfolding power of the Great White Spirit, then the centre of which we speak begins to radiate light; and if you are truly, quietly attuned, it can suffuse the whole aura with healing; with cleansing and healing. And then you will say, 'I feel in the pink!' To feel in the pink means that your aura is radiating a soft pink light, and this is giving it health. Thus it is that those who are feeling 'in the pink', as you put it, are, perhaps unconsciously, continually healing or helping others to heal themselves. They will come into a room where there is depression and confusion and disease, and they will smooth out the inharmonies. They raise the vibrations, they give out healing and then after such a person has gone, the others will say, 'I feel much better for so-and-so's visit!'

This is the kind of healing which, in a far greater way, initiates and Masters give forth.

We hope that those who seek spiritual healing in whatever form will not make the mistake of leaving their healing entirely to the healer. True healing must be co-operative. It used to be said that the patient must have faith. But faith is not just a dependence upon an outside power, it is an inward knowing. This means that the patient must seek communion with spiritual companions and with Christ, or the Christ spirit. And when the patient opens heart and mind to the great light of Christ, then the healing forces truly enter into the soul and the body.

The healer is really the amplifier of that power. All of us are at times unable to attune ourselves sufficiently strongly or completely to the power of the Great White Spirit; and then the healer becomes the amplifier of that power, and is able to make the contact with the patient, to help the patient to help himself.

There are times during earthly life when the body gets heavy to carry and the path becomes wearisome. We would like to help you at such times, and we can help you if you allow us to. This means that you should turn your thoughts away from the bondage of earth and the physical body, and look into the heights, to the mountain tops, where there is peace and strength and life eternal.

When you are raised to that higher plane of spiritual realisation, how small your material cares seem to you! Indeed they do not seem real at all, and all physical disability recedes into the background. Now if you could always maintain your contact with the spiritual level of life you would find that your earthly life would become healthy, holy, harmonious. We know that it is very easy for us to talk like this, but you also know, brethren, that when on rare occasions you do make that true contact with the life of spirit all inharmony and pain falls away from you and you live for that brief moment in an ecstasy of spiritual happiness. This is perhaps what the Master Jesus was trying to teach you when he said, 'I and my Father are one . . . The Father that dwelleth in me, he doeth the works'. It is not beyond the power of any soul to touch that realm of harmony and perfectness.

Now, my children, when you are faced with problems and perplexities, seek first the kingdom of heaven, the kingdom of God, seek daily contact with the source of your spiritual and physical being. Create in imagination your own private chapel – you can make it very beautiful – and then kneel in simplicity before the shrine and ask, and your Father will hear you and the light will shine in your heart; the light will reveal truth to you and show you what to do. Follow the true light, not the light of your own desire. Lay your desires on one side and seek in simplicity and in truth. The light will guide you. Be strong in the light.

He who would Heal . . .

Life is one whole. But in order for man to see and feel and know this truth, and to bring it right through into his physical life, he must first make his own contact in the silence, in the stillness, with the heart of truth symbolised for you by the Christ Star. Now, Christ is more than a person; Christ is love; Christ is a quality of consciousness that can come to all men.

This is important in healing. Jesus, before attempting to heal, would shut away all noise, all confusion and chatter of the material plane. They were all put outside. You too do this before you come into your healing sanctuary. You leave outside your personal worries; you leave outside all controversial thought, you close the doors of the Lodge of your soul against all interruption. You do not allow the voice of your mind or of your lower self to argue with you and say that what you are doing is a waste of time; you concentrate your whole being on the Star, the Christ heart, love. 'The Father that dwelleth in me, he doeth the works.' The Father is working through me. You know this truth, but it helps you when we come and repeat it to you again and again. When we come, we do so to help you to make your contact with the Star, with the Christ sphere, with the love, so that you have no doubt, no fear in your mind. You *know*, because you have seen and you have felt.

When doubting Thomas averred that he would not believe unless he put his fingers in the prints of the nails in the Master's hands and thrust his hand in the side pierced by the sword, of course it was the material mind speaking, that mind which still speaks today, asking for physical proof of spiritual truth. And my children, so often when people are healed they quickly forget it. Sometimes they think they have been healed by material means. They forget so quickly. We know! . . . we look down on our beloved earthly brethren, and see how quickly they forget their healing – not always, but sometimes. But Jesus took no notice of that weakness of the flesh. He kept on and on faithfully, even to restoring the ear of the soldier who had come to arrest him in the garden. Jesus was all forgiveness and love – unfailing in his healing.

Keep on Keeping On

When we speak of acceptance, we mean that healers and patients alike must accept what comes. If the patient does not immediately respond to the healing rays do not be despondent, accept the way that God ordains. If the patient does not recover in a flash, do not lose your faith; keep quietly on, dear patient, keep quietly on, dear healer. There is a process of manifestation – that is the best word we can find – the soul-manifestation of the spirit of holiness in the patient, and this spirit of holiness is what brings health. Healing must take place from the foundation. Sometimes it is a long time working through into manifestation. There are occasions when it manifests in a flash, that is because the soul is ready for that sudden healing; but it is not for everyone. Usually it is a slow process, the spiritual power works slowly but surely: it is difficult for the earthly mind to comprehend the workings of the spirit. Nevertheless, that healing power commences to work. In some instances, the healing power has to get through a very hard crust, and then it has to work its way up just like a plant making its way up from the dark earth into the sunlight above the earth.

We know that our dear earthly brethren cannot bear to see a loved one suffering, but we would tenderly point out that man does not always know better than God, his Creator. When a loved one has to go through certain experiences which are painful, perhaps a painful transition from the physical life, men on earth do not know what is at the same time being given to that apparently suffering soul. We want you to remember this, because in so many cases, when the physical body appears to be suffering, the soul is raised up into the heavens; can be experiencing the most beautiful happiness.

We assure you that God is love, and his law is all love, no matter what you may see on the earth. The Great White Spirit looks upon that suffering with tender mercy. You may not be able to see this, but you do not know what is taking place in the invisible. What appears to be suffering is so often something quite the reverse from the spiritual side of life. All healers should remember this.

Of course this does not mean that you should leave people to suffer. Always do what you can do to make a patient or another person easy in mind, comfortable in body. Always be kind and loving. Jesus, the great healer and teacher, gave the parable of the good Samaritan, who tended the wounds of the man who had been cruelly attacked and then left by the wayside to die. And the good Samaritan came and bore that individual to a place where he could be tenderly cared for. Remember this, the good Samaritan who always looks to see what he can do to ease the burden of any suffering, whether it is the suffering through sickness of the body, or suffering in the soul.

Breathing in the Light

One of the finest methods of which we can tell you for the strengthening of the finer bodies and the nervous system is by deep breathing. People so little realise the importance of breathing correctly, and consequently there is a continual introduction into the physical body and subtler bodies of a certain amount of poisonous matter, through the wrong method of breathing and thought. For it is not only the intake of breath, but the intake of etheric and spiritual atoms which prejudices or encourages the health of the body.

We suggest this simple exercise: on rising, face the Sun, if possible before an open window (which should have been open all night). Stand erect so that you are correctly polarised, with the spine straight, the solar plexus controlled, heels together, toes slightly apart. Before you inhale, centre your whole concentration upon the light, upon the Sun. As you become enfolded by and absorb the golden rays of the Sun, the Great Spirit, Father–Mother God, you will feel in your heart a sense of loving dependence upon the Father–Mother. Try to realise your relationship with the Great White Spirit. Now take your breath; and as you breathe, realise that you are breathing not only air but very life-atoms into your being. Raise your arms as you breathe in, if you find it helpful, and then as you breathe out let your arms fall slowly. You breathe in and absorb this stream of life and light from the Father–Mother God, and then you let it fall from you in blessing upon others. So you absorb God's life, and you bless all life. You receive and you give; and so you come into harmony with the rhythmic life-stream. It will feed your nerves, and give you a sense of peace and control.

After doing this exercise for two or three days, don't then say, 'I am too late, I cannot do it'. You must discipline yourself until your daily communion will become so natural that you would not miss it; it will become an automatic action, and you will thus become *en rapport* with the universal life-force, as was your brother Indian in those days of long ago.

Deep breathing brings an inner tranquillity, a steadiness and valuable help in facing any ordeals which lie ahead. A Master never allows himself to become flustered or worried; a Master can face anything with perfect calm.

A Healing Meditation

Beloved brethren, we ask you to endeavour to forget your particular pains. Do not concentrate on your symptoms. We understand how you feel and the difficulty you have in discarding your awareness of your particular symptom, but we come from the world of spirit to bring you love, and to help you to realise the presence of invisible helpers and spiritual power. Of ourselves we cannot heal. No mortal can do this. We all look to the source of all life and power, and to be healed you too must look to that source. We can help you but *you* have to learn, have to learn to heal yourselves. You have to surrender your physical bodies and your souls and your wills to the infinite power of Christ's love.

To help you to do this we are going to describe to you the scene as we see it from the spirit world. We would help you to rise in spirit into the Temple of Healing in the spiritual spheres. Now remember that this state of consciousness is real and eternal; it is more real than your physical life. You have been led into a temple of healing. The fabric of the temple is pure white and contains all the rays of the Christ light. We are in the centre of a large circle of angelic beings. Our temple is open on all sides to nature, to a sunlit country garden. Flowers are there, fountains and running brooks.

Centre your thoughts upon these things. This is a true description of the Temple of Healing in the world of spirit. Above our heads is a jewel, a star. It is cut in a very special way so that the rays from the Sun which penetrate it shine through in different colours. The pure white ray is split up into many different colours and according to your need you will select one or more of these rays. Do not think of your particular symptoms. We repeat this. Just surrender your whole being to the rays of the spiritual Sun. That spiritual Sun is the heart of the great being, Christ, the Lord of earth's humanity. He brings to you the bread of life, the cosmic body of the Son. Take, absorb this bread. It will feed you, nourish you, sustain you . . .

He brings you the cup of golden liquid, the wine, his life-force. Drink . . .

I AM the way to life.

I AM divine peace . . . divine peace . . . divine peace.

I AM divine love . . . divine love . . . divine love.

I AM within your heart. Heal thyself, O brother.
Amen.

V

'I am the True Vine'

The Meaning of Holy Communion

IN THE FIRST chapter of this book we stressed the simple, human way in which White Eagle always spoke. He often said that however much a person read, or listened to teaching, it was in the light and love that he endeavoured to unveil in his own heart, that he would find truth. And so the way he talks helps us to find the space and the simplicity to make our own communion with the Great White Spirit. The word 'communion' is often applied just to a particular ceremony in the Christian church, but perhaps any moment of true attunement to the world of light, when we enter the quiet within and become receptive to the presence of love, can be called communion. This was certainly the sense in which White Eagle often used the word. However, he often invoked the symbols given by the Master Jesus for man's communion with the Christ spirit; and spoke with great reverence of their profundity and beauty.

This chapter concerns the interpretation White Eagle has given of the symbols of the bread and the wine – although we feel sure that he himself would not wish to lay claim to have given the only understanding possible. He would say he was trying to help us understand in our own being just a little of the life of God to which these symbols point.

In White Eagle's teaching, the place of true communion is the heart. He says that really to understand what communion means we have to learn to enter what he calls 'the temple of the heart'. Although this place of quietness within, and of communion with the spiritual life, is always within every man, it tends to become obscured in human life by the demands of the personality, and so we have to learn afresh to turn within. It does help us to enter 'the temple of the heart' about which White Eagle speaks, if in daily life we learn the art of letting go with the outer mind, and if we take the trouble regularly to let the outer self become quiet. Really we need to learn to release the tight hold we all have with the outer self and outer mind on the complexities of human life. This does not mean at all ceasing to be practical, but it does mean learning inner quietness and surrender. As we do this we allow the inner life, the life of the heart and of love to become strong. And it will be easier for us too to follow White Eagle when he says, as so often, that in order to enter the temple of the heart 'you withdraw from the clamour of the outer world of man, and the outer world of your own mind'.

White Eagle once drew a parallel between entering a place of worship, and entering into a higher consciousness. This will help prepare the way for the understanding he gives us of communion, which takes place most fully in the higher consciousness of man. He spoke of the familiar words of Jesus:

You sometimes listen to the simple words of Jesus, 'Abide ye in my love'. Can you comprehend the profundity of these words, 'Abide ye in my love'?

Now, when you come into this Lodge* you will admit that you feel a different atmosphere; you respond to a different level of consciousness from that prevailing in the outer world. This you can understand because you have experienced it. You will recognise through your own experience that there is a harder world outside, so often in conflict, and an inner and more gentle world when you come into this Lodge. This will serve as an illustration of what takes place when you enter your own inner lodge. By this we mean that you should endeavour to close the doors of the outer mind and the outer self and seek through earnest aspiration to find and enter the temple of the heart, the spirit. Through your love for God you will find you are able to create in your imagination a place of beauty, the highest and best which your mind can conceive. You may even have been helped to 'build up', as we

* These words were spoken in the White Eagle Lodge.

say, to create in your highest and most godly imagination, a temple of great beauty, of whiteness, of architectural perfection. Then you become aware of light: you become aware of intense and prevailing peace; and also you are aware of invisible companions. Deep within a voice tells you that you are in the company of gentle white brethren. You may not see them, not as you expect to see them, but nevertheless you *feel* these loving brethren of your spirit are with you. Your heart is touched by an invisible beauty and love. You cannot explain it, but you just *know*. You know what you are then registering is eternal truth, you are touching the truth of the infinite and eternal life of God.

'Abide ye in my love.' This is exactly what you are doing when you enter that higher level of conscious awareness of divine love. When you can frequently and at suitable times enter this higher consciousness, this temple of the spirit, you will each time get a little stronger spiritually, a little more certain of the power of your own spirit, and of divine spirit.

*

To some people who are unfamiliar with White Eagle's teaching, it may seem a little difficult to understand why he so frequently talks of using the imagination; but in a service of worship, perhaps while he was speaking, it was so easy to feel that one was being 'helped to build up, to create in one's highest and most godly imagination, a temple of great beauty'. He would bring a feeling of great blessing, helping everyone to become aware of their attunement with the simple spirit of love, the Christ spirit. In this spirit of worship which he helped us feel, such 'imagination' just seemed a natural extension of loving – because in a way such a 'temple of the spirit' *is* just the simple love and worship and aspiration of everyone's hearts. It is as White Eagle has so often said: 'love is light'. When he describes such a temple it is just a way of helping our hearts to make a bridge to the world of light.

On occasions such as a service of worship, it is not just one individual seeking attunement; each is, perhaps subtly, very much part of a group. The joining together – in a sense the ritual of joining together – in a service of worship or in meditation does help each one to become a little more open to the higher consciousness, and to hold the communion in the silence of their own heart. Of course, White Eagle's words based on the saying 'Abide ye in my love' apply just the same when we are on our own. However, the actual symbols given by Jesus, of the partaking of the bread and the wine, do suggest an at-one-ment and brotherhood in the greater life of the spirit; and thus it seems particularly fitting that in our approach to this communion we should be working together with others. In the light of White Eagle's words about entering one's own inner lodge we can perhaps now understand him more deeply when he speaks of a communion of spirit. In these words (spoken at the end of a service) he is surely showing the spirit of the saying, 'Where two or three are gathered together in my name, there am I in the midst of them':

Now by the side of every one of you is a guide, a helper. This chapel is a blaze of gold . . . In the centre is the presence of the Lord Christ. He has come to each one of you in the silence of your own heart, in your own inner temple, the simple white temple.

He offers you the symbols of the bread and the wine, of holy communion with him – the bread symbolising the whole of creation.

'My cosmic body:' he says; 'take it; eat; be at one with me. Sip from my cup the divine essence, divine love. *Be* love, even as I am love. Give love, and know the true peace of heaven. Peace . . .'

*

Although White Eagle talks of entering the 'upper room' in order to hold communion, this doesn't mean that these symbols of the spirit refer to something withdrawn or apart from everyday life. In ordinary active life we can be touched by the radiance of this communion: when, perhaps with sacrifice, we are able to act with real practical kindness and love; when we see for a moment in someone the light of a selfless love; when we find we can do our work for its own sake, as a form of service, White Eagle says we are approaching the same thing – approaching, perhaps quite unconsciously, the divine life. He once said:

You have the words of Christ, 'I am the bread of life'. We assure you that you take this bread and you eat it when you live in service to your brother man. This is the absorption into your being of the bread of life. By your brotherhood and your kindly service in the world you are partaking of the bread of communion with other souls and with the Christ.

As you receive the light, give it; and you cannot give without receiving, for as you give you are already receiving the beauty, the glory of the Christ spirit.

He has also said that it will help us understand what is meant by the wine if we think of that sweet essence which is born into the heart through human experience – above all through the experience of love, which brings both happiness and joy, and suffering and renunciation. It is a little as if in physical life we are made to feel the squeezing of the grapes, but through this squeezing the heart gains understanding of life, strength and compassion, and becomes able to hold the sweet essence . . . the simple human heart that reflects divine love.

We have to realise that the references in the teaching of Jesus to the bread 'which cometh down from heaven' and the wine, which (according to the tradition handed down in St John's gospel) some of his hearers found difficult to understand, are living images for the divine life, of our relationship with the divine life. Their significance will always be wider and greater than anything we can neatly harness with our minds. These images were surely Jesus' way of putting profound truth simply and purely, of actually conveying mystical awareness that his listeners could receive. Jesus himself said, after talking of the bread 'which cometh down from heaven', 'The words that I speak unto you, they are spirit, and they are life'. It is similar when we come across the saying, 'He that eateth my flesh, and drinketh my blood, dwelleth in me, and I in him'. White Eagle says that on occasions such as this, Jesus was speaking as the great and pure vehicle of the Christ. It is as he says in an earlier chapter, 'And when we learn to love and recognise that simple, gentle, tender form, then we open the way for the greater light, the glorious Christ light'. 'Drinking the blood' White Eagle perhaps explained most clearly when he interpreted another phrase from the bible:

When the phrase, 'Washed in the blood of the Lamb' is used in orthodox religion, we want you always to interpret these words as 'purified by the divine love of the Son', because this is really

91

what is meant. The blood is the life-force, the life-force of the Great Healer, the Lord Christ, and his life-force was that of love, and the most purifying and healing essence that man can have and know.

Eating the flesh (or the bread) really means absorbing the substance of the Christ light, the white ether as White Eagle sometimes calls it, into our being; and through taking this light into our hearts, having our consciousness opened to the true, the Christ life. He that 'eateth my flesh and drinketh my blood' has found in his heart a little of the universal Christ-consciousness.

In our own meditation or service of communion we are touching in a very simple way on a great mystery, just catching a glimpse of something that really has to be felt to be understood – and before which we are surely all as children. White Eagle makes us feel that when we are truly able to receive the bread (and this is there for every living soul to take) there comes to us the intuition, the consciousness that we are not separate, but part of that great spiritual life. When the heart truly opens to the Christ blessing, the Christ love, our awareness can be drawn beyond the veils of illusion that cling so strongly to the physical life. It is in this awareness of brotherhood in the greater life of the spirit that we realise that we are fed by that light which sustains all physical life; which sustains the whole. The bread 'is a symbol of his cosmic body which is everywhere and for everyone to take and eat thereof when they are in the spirit' – or in the higher consciousness. The secret of all lies in the Christ spirit in the heart, and it is the purpose of communion to stimulate the Christ-consciousness in man.

When White Eagle talks of the picture of Jesus giving the cup he suggests that this is the symbol, in human form – a true symbol, an embodiment – of that great giving of love from the Christ heart into the heart of all creation – but which it is the destiny of the human soul to receive consciously. The cup is the symbol of the heart, and when the Christ gives the cup it is the outpouring from his heart which touches the I AM in the heart of every man and woman, every soul. White Eagle once said, 'Think in terms of the many and the One; think of the many in the One, and the One in the many, and you will get some idea of the true communion'. In this giving of the divine life into the heart, the grail cup, of every man, that individual life becomes attuned again to the universal life, has its being more fully in that life of which we are all a part. In the giving of the wine the individual life does not lose its distinctness, it becomes more truly individual by being drawn back into at-one-ment, completion with the whole.

The ceremony of communion is almost like a dance about the King of Love, who gives himself, his very heart, 'that they may all be one' and compounded of love, his very substance.

*

We have tried to draw from White Eagle's teaching a picture of true communion. It is the beauty of White Eagle's teaching that he shows us that this great mystery, although it concerns the universal life, is also something very simple, something in the human heart. The awareness of the greater life of which he speaks has – if it is to grow – to find expression in the simple details of everyday life. He once talked of this beautifully when he said:

'I am the bread of life': the deep-within-you, the I AM in you, Christ in you, is the bread of life . . . partake of that bread, the bread of Christ . . . the wine and the bread of Christ which is within your own inner sanctuary . . . and peace be with you . . . surrender to God, and all will be well.

You know, my brethren, this spirit of Christ is not a pious, sanctimonious spirit, it is a very human, kindly, sympathetic, understanding spirit. It is not long-faced, it is cheery, it is tactful, it is kind, it is a giving-forth from the whole being of goodwill, love, companionship. You know what we mean.

A Prayer

(THIS PRAYER was given by White Eagle at a service for spiritual healing, as were the words of the meditation which follows:)

May we come into the presence of the Most High, the holy and blessed Trinity: Father, Mother and Son, the Christ. We withdraw from the material life. We lay aside all our material and physical burdens, and as white-robed candidates for initiation into the mysteries of heaven, we come. O Great White Spirit, we pray that we may be able to receive the blessings of thy life. May the angel presences be able to make themselves felt here with each one of us. May the bridge between the physical life and the spiritual life be built from our love and faith, nay our certainty of the invisible life. May we partake of the communion with spirit, the bread and the wine of life.   *Amen.*

We want you to remember always to reach up into the spiritual life and to bring into your earthly life the gentleness and the beauty of your real nature, your spiritual nature, which is part of the divine nature, part of God. As the Master Jesus said to his hearers, 'Be ye therefore perfect, even as your Father which is in heaven is perfect'. He meant, know in your innermost being that you *are* perfect in the Father God. He said, 'I and my Father are one'. He teaches all his brethren on earth to follow this path of truth, to realise that they and the Father *are* one; and that God is the creator of all life and he is in you, and you have the power within you to create, and your goal is the creation of the perfect life on earth through the realisation of the perfectness of your spirit which is at one with the Father.

We raise your consciousness, dear earthly brethren, we raise you with us far away and above the discord and the disease of the earth.

Come with us into that perfect state of spiritual life where there is no sickness, no disharmony, no darkness.

Let us partake in spirit of the bread of life, the bread which is the cosmic substance which the Father has sent down to his children, the substance by which they live, by which they create perfection.

The figure of the Master is in your midst, brethren. He stands in the centre. He is in the glory of the heavenly light. He is shining. He holds up his hands and brings into our vision the white bread, the white ether. 'O Father–Mother God, we thank thee for this bread of life and for thy blessing. May these thy children who take and eat this bread be sustained by the bread of life.' He breaks it into pieces and offers it to you, to each one of you. Take the bread and eat the heavenly food, and pray as you do so for deeper understanding of this age-old ritual of communion with God.

The cup rests before his heart. It is filled with the juice of the grapes which is the symbol of his spirit. It is the wine of life. It is full of power. Then he thanks his Father–Mother God for this life, for this wine, this eternal spirit, which is man's succour through eternal life. Drink of this spirit. We are all one in this divine spirit of our Father–Mother God. New life fills your being. The light pours through your soul. The healing power cleanses and perfects you in God.

VI

Sayings of the Christ within

THE FOLLOWING short passages are not necessarily meant to be read in sequence; each is almost a meditation in itself. They all lead us quietly to deeper understanding of the philosophy and way of life to which White Eagle opens our vision – the 'the way of the Christ within'.

A Little Child Shall Lead Them

To become as a little child means that there must be a transference from thinking in the brain to feeling and intuition in the heart centre. Then the little child, the spirit of humility in your heart, will listen, and it will also teach the mind in the head. You have the saying of the great seer and poet Isaiah: 'A little child shall lead them'. Such prophetic sayings and all the sayings of Jesus, whilst they have an outward application, also have an esoteric meaning – they come from within, and irradiate the without. So also from within the heart the deepest truth can radiate and manifest in simple practical kindness and love on the physical plane of life. Thus 'A little child shall lead them' . . . Christ, the child which

97

resides in the centre of the heart – the heart centre, which is the centre of your universe.

Listen to the Master within

Man makes his life so complex; he brings upon himself an avalanche of confusion, pain and suffering; he is driven by desires of the mind and of the body, both enslaving him. Yet the way to freedom is simple, so simple that most pass it by. Learn to listen to the voice of the Master within. So often men will not listen to the still small voice of their Master, or they cannot recognise his voice. Or sometimes what they think to be the voice of their Master is only the voice of self, and self expresses itself in many ways – self-importance, self-love, wishing to shine before other men. All these are of the lower self. But the voice of the Master in man does not indulge in these emotions; it is gentle, selfless, at peace – at peace because it knows God.

The soul setting forth on the spiritual path can become absorbed in its own progress, or become inflated with its own spiritual grandeur and power. But if the soul has striven with all its might to follow in the footsteps of Christ; if a man has endeavoured truly to absorb the gentle humility of the Christ, he can never lose himself in self-glorification, for then he knows that he is neither great nor wonderful, that of himself he could not heal, teach or give comfort. He knows that any good flowing through him is of the Christ, is of God. The test, dear ones, is that of the Christ spirit; and if you can truly feel that the gentle, humble spirit of the Son of God is walking by your side, your hand in his, you cannot fail.

Acceptance

We would assure you that as you daily strive to set aside all the resentment and fear of the lower self, you will be getting nearer to that expansion of your own consciousness wherein you will feel and be blessed with heavenly joy and comfort and assurance. So many of you are frustrated in your daily life because things will not go the way you want them to go. You want things to be different from what they are, when what the true aspirant is after is that complete acceptance of the wisdom of God's laws.

Love is the Divine Transmuter

In the world there is too much haste; there is no calm, no period of retirement from the battle of life. Some of you are so eager to get on with a particular plan that you feel yourself frustrated by any halt. You become filled with a kind of fever; and maybe when you are told to be patient you say to yourself, 'But the spirit people don't understand the needs of the flesh and the demands of the earthly life'.

My brother, my sister, we in spirit understand only too well the claims of the physical life, for we have, stored up in our souls, experiences such as you are even now undergoing. So when you are told to *make* time to withdraw from feverish activity, remember that those who proffer this advice have learned the need for this withdrawal; for surely, surely only in the secret places will man make contact with the source of his being; only in the secret places can he truly pray.

We speak as one of you, we suffer as you suffer. The thought comes to us: 'But why should you, a spirit, suffer because we suffer?' Because, my brethren, love gives us understanding, it makes us feel with you, as you feel. Yet although we feel with you, and understand you, and absorb from you your heartaches, your sorrows do not weigh us down, because love is the divine transmuter. Love is the alchemist which transmutes the base metal of earthliness, the pain and passions of earth. Love transmutes all this, absorbs it into itself, changes it into pure gold.

This is why you feel strengthened after contact with your guide, and you know that all is well. Your guide has brought you the light and love of God which reigns supreme in the heavenly state, and you are uplifted and strengthened and blessed by it. But you have to learn for yourself to receive the cup and transmute the experience of your earthly life.

You are Free

We would say a word about the corruptible little earthly mind, through which man suffers, although he does not always know it whilst he is chained to the life of the physical body. Man is chained; but it is his work, it is his opportunity, to release himself from his own chains. Do you remember the miracle of the disciple who was imprisoned, who was limited and chained to the prison-house on earth? The angels came and touched the chains, and they fell away, and the disciple walked out of his prison.

We would interpret this by saying: when you allow the angels to come to touch your soul, your inner self, when you can realise the presence of the angels and the Christ presence within you, the chains of the physical life, and the chains of the earthly mind, begin to fall away. Your spirit is free and you go forth from your prison-house.

Healers of Men

Do not be dragged down into the vortex of mental and emotional conflict by the troubles of those around you, but try to understand their need and help them to help themselves, not by preaching to them but by striving to be like your Master, inwardly gentle, kind and patient. 'I am the way; I am the truth; I am the life.' The Christ behind and within you is the I AM, the AUM, the life.

Be not disappointed, dear earthly children, if you cannot achieve exactly what you want when you want it. Oh do strive for that quiet, patient spirit! Attune yourselves to the Christ, going into the silence, giving thanks, not asking for anything, but giving thanks for what you have already received, what you know you are receiving. This is faith. Give thanks and you will find faith and faith will make you whole. Faith will make all crooked places straight. Forgive others. Forgive, and you are instantly forgiven, and there is no soul who does not need forgiveness. Forgive, and you shall be forgiven. If you are over-anxious, feeling you are not being given the work that you want to do, feeling that you are overcharged with power and you could do so much more than opportunity is given to you to do, we would remind you that you cannot choose, not necessarily, the particular path you want. You stand before your Master awaiting his orders. This is the true way. Be spontaneous; be simple; above all be full of love. Make no demands, my children. Just be a servant of God.

The Rose of the Christ Life

When you were breathed forth from the Creator, the divine seed was planted in your soul; and it is expected that you will, in the course of life's experiences in many incarnations, develop and unfold the rose of the Christ life. This can only be done by love, by the soul learning to love God and all God's creation. But this lesson, dear brethren, must be learnt whilst the soul is manifesting through physical matter. The physical plane is your school. Never be eager to get away from your physical life. Guard it; protect your body; make your body healthy and strong. Pray that you may live long in the land of the physical world, because in this state of life the soul expands and grows in wisdom and love.

The Self and the Selfless

We know that there are many teachers on your earth who are speaking and urging individualism, the importance of individual development. We do not decry this, but we suggest that in the Aquarian Age there is a fuller understanding necessary for man. While each soul is a unit and must develop, within its capacity, its own inner strength, along with the development of that individual strength there must also be the unfoldment of the great spirit, the Christ spirit, so that there is not merely individualism, there is universalism. The brotherhood is endeavouring to help humanity to understand and to develop the universal Christ love.

The unit must eventually become completely absorbed into the whole – and yet it still retains its individuality; it may help you to think of the grain of said on the shore. Few have got as far as developing the self into the selfless. Be strong in the self, but be stronger in the selfless.

Follow the Star

The more awakened a soul, the more quickly does it recognise love in its simple and possibly crude form in its brother man. This is our work, brothers – to observe, understand and become unified with that love-quality which we should recognise instantly in the living soul of our brother. We agree with you that we may be disappointed at the outset; we may even look at some souls with despair and think they are bereft of love, but this is erroneous thought. In every living soul there is love, but it is often covered up under many layers. It will depend upon the power of the light which we ourselves can direct from our heart, whether we shall see the love in our brother's soul.

We have said that the heart of man can be likened to a torch-light on a dark night. Your heart centre can cast a beam of light into the darkened byways. From this beam you will discern the souls dwelling in the shadows. We are not speaking from a plane divorced from scientific thought or truth. We speak as one of you, because in the work of the brotherhood we become united in spirit. There is no separation, and we who have for the time being laid down the physical body and taken another, we identify ourselves with you, with your physical life.

In the work of brotherhood, we should identify ourselves with the whole of humanity. Inwardly there should be no separation between us and our brothers, no matter what their class, creed, colour or race – we are all one. We must aspire to this realisation of the universal life.

The Star is the symbol of perfect life, perfect balance; the symbol of the Christ man, of the Son of God. This six-pointed Star, the Star of Bethlehem, is the Star of love and it is a Star of true peace. Such peace is not a static thing, but powerful.

Peace is true love, without restraint.

Peace in the soul, peace in the consciousness, is creative in a perfect, gentle and harmonious way.

The Star of Bethlehem that we worship, salute and bow before . . . is the keynote of human happiness.

Through the Eyes of the Master

We would bring to you, dear brethren, a vision of the Master whom you follow. He is a majestic figure; he is so tall and noble, so shining with pure white light. His earthly brethren are not unknown to him. The face shines with love and the eyes look into each heart with tender compassion. This is truth, my brethren. He is all truth and whatever he sees he loves. He loves you, because he sees in you that shining light, that jewel, which is part of himself.

His hands are raised to bless you . . . and the rays of light fall from his hands, from the tips of his fingers . . . They enter and strengthen your heart. He gives you courage, and joy, and peace.

VII

A Reinterpretation of Traditional Christian Teaching — I

A Talk on True Religion; and the Life of the Master Jesus

WHEN WE come to talk to you, we pray that you may all respond to the influence of the White Brethren who are with us; and above all respond to the pure and sweet influence of the Master, who radiates his love through his brethren of the unseen who are working so closely with humanity.

When we come from the spirit world to talk to you in this way, your vibrations are quickened; the earthly mind sinks into abeyance, and you feel stimulated in spirit. Your heart centre opens like a rose to receive the sweet influences, the wisdom and the beauty of higher spheres of life. This is our purpose when speaking to you from spirit. You may read and hear certain spiritual truths repeated several times. But truth in a sense is always repetitive; it is rather like a wheel, revolving, always bringing to you the same basic law of life.

Yet our purpose is not so much to bring you truth in words, but through these words to stimulate your own spiritual receptivity to unspoken truth which you can only receive in your own way, in your own heart. Not in words alone does truth come, but in the silence, in a pure spiritual atmosphere, in cosmic rays which you can receive more readily in the atmosphere which by your love and service you can create.

We are trying to help you to realise in the silence of your own heart a little of this pure truth from God, your Creator. We are trying to help you to realise the divine presence . . . God in you, God in all creation. God is and ever has been. From the heart of God all creatures have been born. God animates all matter and causes it first to become, then to grow and to evolve.

The Word was sound, vibration, and the vibration created by the Word started life in form. The scriptures of the world all contain this same truth, they all tell of the Word, the sound, the vibration, the activity of the atom which created form or life on the earth. This is the beginning of life in the universe; then when mortal life has run its course, there comes a turning inward, a withdrawal from that outer manifestation.

When man has become cognisant of this divine law, and of this essence, God, in the heart and centre both of his own being and of the whole universe, then he realises that he is not separate but part of the whole, and part of God, and God is in him; thus slowly he merges into this greater consciousness, into the *all*-ness of life.

This is the stage when brotherhood of the spirit, brotherhood of all life, is realised by man. When, in the deep silence, man knows God, he knows all. 'Man, know thyself'; know the God, know this beauty, this life, within the silence, and thou shalt know . . . all.

Thou shalt know the universe in which thou livest.

This basic and simple truth is inherent in all true religions in different forms; in all good, true men and women there is this heart of divine love. When the critical earthly mind and analytical faculty gets to work, that sweet, pure truth becomes covered up; and the brain of man, instead of being his servant, becomes his dictator. The earthly mind has a capacity for concealing the real; therefore man has to become very strong in his conviction and in his devotion to the Father–Mother God. It is the narrowing of the vision of truth which eventually covers it up. Truth can never be destroyed, but it can become so deeply buried that for a time it is lost to the sight of those active only at the worldly level of consciousness.

Every religion has been introduced to humanity by a Master or great initiate. When that teaching was first spoken through the lips of the teacher it was simple and pure, but when after a time it was elaborated by the mind of its adherents, it sometimes became distorted.

However, the age of Aquarius, when the World Teacher will become active, is now with us. His influence will manifest not so much in organised and established religions and churches (which will gradually change from their present form) but in the spirit, in the truth, working like leaven in the bread, which will lighten the whole world. It will manifest in groups, and in the urge towards freedom, towards a better way of life, to which mankind is now responding – the urge for a more harmoniously organised life; not a lazy life, but a more harmonious life which will afford man the opportunity to develop spiritually.

It is difficult for man to reach up and respond to the divine spirit when he is imprisoned in the hard rock of earthly materialism, or in a diseased body. Until through his spirit man understands the law of God, and works in harmony with it, until he has attained a degree of self-discipline, his whole being is unbalanced; he lacks ease and peace of mind; he is in the thraldom of emotional and mental conflict. How do you think the adepts, the initiates, retain a physical body long after the recognised human life-span? How do they retain their youthful appearance? How can they wield that power which demonstrates their complete control over the physical atoms? Only because, through many, many incarnations, and by practising the divine laws of life, they have achieved mastery. They are able to manipulate and control matter on the physical plane and on the higher levels of life. When a highly developed soul understands spiritual science and can work in harmony with divine law, he is able to perform what is called a miracle.

You will wonder what all this has to do with you personally. You will say: 'But we are very far from adeptship, very far from understanding the divine law which controls matter'. Yes, but the reason we say these things is just to open your minds to your infinite possibilities and the power which is within you. But the God in you will only be developed and brought through to full capacity by your own effort.

The life of Jesus was the most wonderful demonstration of divine love and the perfecting of the truth of God-in-man; Jesus was the perfect channel for the light of God. But we want you to realise the difference between the simple, pure teaching which flowed through Jesus of Nazareth from his Father–Mother God, and the later religion organised and dictated by brilliant scholars of the time. Ponder on the sayings and parables of Jesus and you will see how simple, pure and profound were all the illustrations which he took from everyday life to teach his

111

disciples the great truths of life. We try, in perhaps a simple way, to repeat to you the basic truths which came to you through Jesus: that God is in man; that the love of God works through man; that God in man gives him power to heal, the power to overcome death.

Why do you think Jesus raised the dead to life? It was to teach those who came after that man himself can attain mastery over matter, and that death has no real existence, only in men's minds.

We know quite well your arguments; you say: 'But death is round us all the time!' May we suggest to you that man himself is the cause of his own death? It is not God's will that man should die. Man brings about his own death, by his ignorance, by the unconscious breaking of divine law. When divine law is fully working in man, there can be no decay. There may be a change of form, but we do not use the word 'decay' (although in what man regards as decay there is a deep spiritual principle at work). When ignorance is replaced by knowledge, the body will be retained as long as it is needed; there will come instead a quickening of the vibrations of the physical atoms, which will lead to the transition of the body to a higher plane of activity. Do not imagine that the forms you see in meditation or in clairvoyance are just wispy imaginary forms; they are solid and real, and to those who are functioning at that level, of course the lower forms look wispy and unreal. You, in the physical sense, are not nearly so real and solid as you think you are.

Picture Jesus seated with a group of his disciples or followers, teaching them the simple ways of God, the way that God wishes his earthly children to live so that they may overcome evil and death. Think of him on a hilltop, with his disciples about him, speaking not of himself but of the Father which dwelt in him. The divine spirit, pure spirit, came down from heaven into the heart of Jesus, speaking simple and pure truth to his disciples, as pure religion has always come through into the mind and soul of the teacher – not from the mental level but from the spirit.

We have spoken of man overcoming death, and we must answer a question which has arisen in the minds of some of you: 'Then what about the crucifixion of Jesus?' Why was Jesus crucified on the cross, apparently to death? First let us make quite clear to you that Jesus was a willing co-operator with his Father. 'Nevertheless not my will, but thine, be done.' He surrendered to his Father's great purposes, and by his crucifixion a spiritual power baptised the earth, the radiation of which has already lasted for nearly 2,000 years.

The story of the crucifixion of Jesus illustrates that before man can overcome death he must be crucified in himself. Through self-sacrifice, through sacrificing his desires, his hopes, his wishes, his whole being to the will of his Creator, he attains to that supreme degree of mastership which enables him to overcome physical death. First of all there is the surrender, the inner crucifixion through the sinking of the lower self; and then the resurrection into that glorious freedom, the spiritual life which never ends. In that state, when man has overcome his mortal self, he receives the power to command matter, which is what Jesus demonstrated. He raised his body from death and came forth from the tomb, and gave proof to his disciples: 'But I am not dead, I live!' And in that same body he withdrew into the invisible; he changed the atoms again so that he could not be seen by the disciples and those around him, because they were functioning on a lower level, and he at that time was able to function at will on a higher level. The Christian faith is built on this great demonstration. But do not forget that other men, perhaps in lesser degree, have also achieved this mastery over the body, over physical atoms. They have 'gone up in a chariot of fire', or in a great light, and their physical atoms have been transmuted into that higher and more beautiful state of life. We are trying to bring you a vision of the power of the spiritual life that manifested through the life of Jesus.

114

Dear ones of earth, we do not expect miracles from you, but we do say, obey the highest urge in your thoughts and in your life. Armageddon does not take place in a great earthly battle, but within man's own heart, in the battle between his spirit and his lower self. Hold fast to the truth which is struggling for life in your dear human heart. Never lose your vision of the Star, the emblem of the perfect life, balanced, true, always loving.

Jesus and Life After Death

THE QUESTION is often asked, why is it that Jesus apparently gave so little information about the life after death? This seeming omission has puzzled many, who for this reason disbelieve in communion with and communication from those in the higher state of life.

We would endeavour to explain that although Jesus did not specifically refer to the afterlife, nevertheless his whole teaching was to help his followers to comprehend all life – not only in a body on this earth, but life as a whole. People are mistaken when they think of the world of spirit as being something outside, something beyond this present life. We all talk about a life beyond; we use certain words loosely and thereby convey a wrong meaning. But Jesus endeavoured to teach his disciples that there was neither a 'here' nor a 'there', no here or hereafter, but that all life was eternally present, now – God ever-present.

The physical plane, the astral, the etheric, the mental, the celestial – all these planes interpenetrate. You cannot yet fully understand what this means, you are limited by a mental conception as to the nature of space and time, and therefore you cannot recognise the profound truth inherent in the teachings of Jesus.

We speak to you of certain states of consciousness to which man can attain. For instance, you are aware, in the first place, of your physical body. Or, if you wish, you can reach out and become conscious of your emotional body. That is, your emotions may become stirred and desires active. This quickens the astral state of life which is governed by feeling, by emotion. Then again you can reach out above the emotions; you can by an effort of will become active on the higher mental plane. You can even go beyond that mental conception, when the higher emotions come into operation and you become conscious of a heavenly state.

So when you sit to meditate upon spiritual things you usually go through this process of being first conscious of the physical body – which can be very troublesome until you learn to control it by your will. Then your feelings become active, perhaps stimulated by music or by words. Then you are being raised in consciousness, but you are still within yourself. Step by step you go through the varying states of consciousness to the mental and the heavenly. When you once reach the heavenly state, although you are still fully aware of your inner being, of your higher self or your soul, you are also aware of heavenly things. This is made clear to you first of all by light. You feel lighter, more radiant. Something in you activates the physical vehicle, the nervous system. You experience a telepathic communication between the heavenly self or the heavenly state of consciousness and your body. But in the degree you become aware of the body you feel a heaviness, the pull of the earth. This is because you have both stimulated that heavenly consciousness and also linked the heavenly with the earth life. So in time you become pulled back. Yet the one life contains all these states of consciousness.

What happens when you are unable to sustain life in the body any longer? Then the spirit withdraws and the physical body dies, but this physical body is only an envelope or clothing to the spirit. You remain exactly the same as when you had a body attached to your soul and spirit.

Now Jesus, knowing all these things of which we have spoken, was not concerned at all with teaching his disciples about a 'here' and a 'here-after'. He was not wholly concerned with the spirit world; nor yet with the physical or intellectual life or the emotional or celestial life. He was concerned with life *as a whole*. He did not divide it into segments. He had learned the secret of a perfect life. More than this, he had learned the secret of control over all aspects of himself. In him was no separation. The Christ within revealed the whole of life, of universal life. Therefore there was no need for him to speak about a 'hereafter'. To him, death did not exist. Life was eternal.

Christ is Risen

WE WOULD raise your consciousness to the spiritual life, so that you will become aware of the mighty power and gentle presence here with us. The beloved Master Jesus, who was the vehicle or channel for the Christ light and message in the age of Pisces, still works amongst men; particularly amongst those who are sorrowful and in great need. We do not speak idly. We are speaking to certain of you who need the touch of the beloved Jesus, who long for reassurance of his care for you – to you he comes, for he still walks the earth.

We are going to speak to you about the inner significance of the crucifixion, as an experience which awaits every soul on its path of evolution – in fact an experience which you may even now be passing through in your inner selves, and on the inner plane.

'Jesus therefore, knowing all things that should

come upon him' . . . Jesus was a master soul and knew what he must undergo, not only for himself but for all men. For every one of you who undergoes some experience which might be described as a crucifixion, some experience involving great pain and soul-anguish, is doing something for the whole world. Every one who meets such testings of the soul in a resolute and tranquil spirit, even as Jesus did, is raising the vibrations of the whole earth.

The symbol of crucifixion can be found in almost every religion. Indeed we would take you right back in time to the ancient Sun-worship, when the Sun which rose in the heavens was 'crucified' as it passed into darkness; when the coming and going of the seasons, of summer giving place to winter and the Sun being born again with the coming of spring, was thought of as the crucifixion and resurrection of the Sun. The Greek and the Egyptian teachings present the same idea in another form; there was the sacrifice of Osiris, or of Mithras, or of Krishna and other great teachers. Even in the west you have the story of the crucifixion of the American Indian Bird-God, Quetzlcoatl. All these religions tell in symbolic form of the crucifixion of their saviour – for the Sun was then conceived as the saviour of mankind.

We want, however, to get behind this to something deeper. We would not for one moment rob you of your adoration for Jesus the Christ, but rather reinforce both your belief in and knowledge of this great and perfect one who came amongst men to help to save them from pain and suffering. He still comes amongst you to bring you light, and love and joy. He comes to bring you inspiration and spiritual power. But we want you to get an even grander realisation of the Lord Christ. We would impress upon all that the Christ spirit is a cosmic spirit without limitation; Christ is both the spiritual Sun and the Son of God, even as you have been taught.

The crucifixion has an even deeper meaning, which applies to you, for it is indicative of the last of the four great initiations which every human soul must undergo on its journey back to God. It is the earth initiation, which is the culmination of man's life in a physical body, and which was demonstrated to the world in the crucifixion of the Master.

We emphasise that all that the Master Jesus was called upon to face during his crucifixion was endured in a spirit of perfect love. This is the very heart of the spiritual meaning of the earth initiation. In the first place Jesus demonstrated his great love for his fellow man in his attitude towards his betrayer, Judas. Here we would give you two interpretations. One regards Judas as representative of the lower aspect of every man. All of us have a Judas nature in us, and it is this Judas nature which continually denies and betrays our Lord, the Christ spirit within us. Yet there is another interpretation. Jesus recognised in Judas one who had in the past been a victim of betrayal, and his instinct would be to repay that karmic debt with another betrayal. Too often there is retaliation instead of forgiveness, and so the debt is tossed backwards and forwards between the two. But Jesus by his great love drew Judas' debt to himself so that he might forgive him, return love for hate, and so break a sequence which might have gone on for ages. He was remitting the karma of Judas.

In the garden of Gethsemane, you will remember, the disciple Peter struck the soldier with a sword. Jesus immediately healed the wounded man, even though he was apparently his enemy. The whole story of the crucifixion demonstrates, as incident follows incident, the exceeding love in the heart of the Master. He clearly demonstrated that in passing through a spiritual initiation the great need was for love; for the soul to meet all trials, and suffering in a spirit of loving surrender. This is where so many fall short in their attitude towards the difficulties of everyday life. It is natural for the lower self to resent pain and suffering, but when the soul can once surrender to the love of God, accepting without question the wisdom of God's plan, then the soul makes real progress.

This crucifixion of the soul means, in essence, a complete surrender of the lower self. All being surrendered to God, it is then that the soul enters upon the path of mastership.

You may remember the teaching we have given before concerning the transmutation of the very physical atoms of the body to perfect spiritual life. This Jesus demonstrated in his resurrection, and later in his ascension. His body did not die as you understand death, it did not decay. It was recreated and arose purified and glorified, even as every man's body can and will arise in due season. Then Jesus, in full view of his disciples, was caught up into heaven.

There are other great ones who have triumphed over matter, whose bodies have been transformed, illumined, and who have ascended even as Jesus did. These same ·blessed saviours of the world are still alive and active behind the curtain of materiality. You are continually being given proof that the souls of men who have passed out of a body still live on, and can come back and convey their message to you. But it is a different and a far higher thing when the soul becomes so pure and perfected that it can master the very atoms which cause decay and death to the physical body. In this manner the last enemy shall be overcome by the power and the glory of the Christ spirit in man.

As you tread the path of aspiration and endeavour, in due time you will not only see this glory but you will realise it within yourselves. Then at last you will understand the triumph of those words, 'O death, where is thy sting! O grave, where is thy victory!'

We would draw for you a picture of the son of man, the Master Jesus, coming into your midst as a perfected man, as a man warm in humanity, gentle, understanding you and your every need, understanding your problems and difficulties, your disappointments and your fears, yet afire with the light of the Christ spirit. He comes with arms outstretched and is encompassed by shining angels. These are they who have passed through great tribulation, and who are now free, and robed in the glory of the Christ. Yes, Christ is risen! Christ cannot be dead. Christ is life and light and perfection in human and heavenly life.

The Lord, the Great Being, the great vehicle of the Christ spirit glorifies and blesses you, and triumphs with you over the darkness and sorrow of earthly life.

VIII

A Reinterpretation of Traditional Christian Teaching — II

The True Comforter

BELOVED brethren, we speak to you from spirit. You build the etheric bridge and we cross the bridge to you from the world of light to bring you a message of hope, of illumination, love and peace.

When man takes the trouble to withdraw from the conflict of the material world, where there is so much human suffering, and go into the silence of his own soul, it is then that he can receive the message from pure spirit.

We would speak of a time celebrated in your Christian church as Whitsun, the day of Pentecost, upon which the early Christian brotherhood received a demonstration from the heaven world, from the world of light. Remember that the disciples were all sad for they had lost their Master. They had lost the contact with God, with the spiritual life which had given them strength, and the greatest happiness they had known.

They had seen their Master, the beloved Jesus Christ, taken away by ruthless and ignorant men; they had seen him reviled and crucified, and because of this they were broken-hearted and lonely. In the midst of their desolation came this demonstration of the power of the spirit to break through the darkness of sorrow, to break through the gloom and cloud which hung over them. It is an illustration for you all of what can happen to you, too. We understand, dear brethren, your sorrow when a loved one is taken from your side, either by death of the physical body or by mis-understanding; we know how bitter thoughts creep in when the human emotions are stirred, so that you can only feel the anguish of your own grief and you find yourself cut off from the source of spiritual comfort, which is love, which is God. Everything looks black, and it seems as though life itself is fading away from you. But this New Testament story illustrates the vital truth that if you create the right conditions for it, the power of the spirit can break through and fill your heart with love and joy.

The disciples were told to go to Jerusalem and await the coming of their Comforter. Now Jeru-salem is not only a city, it is also a state of consciousness, it indicates a place of light and peace, a place of love. And in that raised state of consciousness the Comforter came to them. The Comforter will come to you too if you will rise in consciousness to a higher level of life, to that 'upper room'. In your thoughts go to that upper room and wait patiently and humbly, in communion with God, and then the Comforter will come to you, 'even the spirit of truth'. Whilst he is dwelling only in his own desires man rejects the Comforter, he cannot and will not be comforted; but when he can surrender all his desires and sorrows and fears into the great love of God, then the spirit of truth comes into man's soul, into his heart, and he is comforted.

Now, let us go back in imagination to that time when the disciples were all gathered together as a brotherhood. We think, and we pass it on to you for your consideration, that Whitsuntide is a particular time of brotherhood, and we would like you to think of it in this way as a time of renewed brotherhood. The brethren 'were all with one accord in one place'. This state of feeling, this gathering together of men and women in one spirit, with one accord, was the religion of the ancient ones, the God-men who came to earth in the beginning to help young humanity to find the way of truth, to find the way to God. And how they taught these young souls was to gather them together at certain times (such as the solstices and equinoxes, and at the time of the full moon when a very special power descends on the earth) and show them how to raise their consciousness to God, and to receive, in that transcendental state of being, the inflow of the cosmic love, the Christ love, into their heart.

So when the early Christian brothers met together they were only following a pattern which they had learnt from their forefathers, this pattern of meeting together for quiet communion and worship of God, giver of all life; worship of the great Mother, the giver of all sustenance.

Man is so involved with his material life, so involved in all the worries and anxieties of the physical life, that he has no time to withdraw from it and attune himself to that beautiful cosmic love which would put all things right on your earth. Men think they must fight for their rights. But Jesus did not teach you this. Jesus taught you to be still . . . to love; the elder brethren, the great Masters of all time and all ages have all taught the same fundamental truth. This does not mean that you do nothing to heal a wound, or to heal the wounds of your fellow men; it means that you practise the law of brotherhood, and by so doing set in motion the power of divine magic which can overcome all darkness. Whatever the conflict, whatever the problem in your life, if you will be patient and give love, give thanks, give forth the spirit of Christ the Son, you will find that the magic will work. Divine magic is the power of brotherhood, the power of the Star, the power of the Christ love, which will make all crooked places straight. This is not a negative thing – it is a very positive state of mind, a state of positive good by which you help the whole world.

And so at Whitsuntide the brethren drew together in one accord, in love. They raised their consciousness to the heavenly life, to the light, and as they waited, and the light poured down into their hearts, they were filled, filled with the joy of life.

Associated with Whitsun is a time of special power, the time of the festival of Christ, when the moon is full in the sign of Gemini. In ancient days the brothers would gather at such times to receive the blessing of this great outpouring of the Christ spirit on earth; through their ceremonies and their contact with the planetary angels they built a vast receptacle, an 'etheric cup' – shall we call it a grail cup? – into which could be seen pouring these great rays of sunlight, the cosmic rays of the Christ life. This was the baptism of the Christ festival.

We suggest that at this time you should use your creative power of imagination and see for yourselves the company of the white brotherhood assembled as they did in those ancient days in the roofless temple high on the plain, awaiting the breaking of the dawn. Hear the music of the spheres playing in harmony with the vibrations of the stones of physical matter. Oh, my children, try to enter this triumphant ceremonial of the

Christ festival . . . see the light flowing over the whole world. See all peoples drawn together in harmony, in love, working to serve – living to give service to all life, and above all to the Creator.

He who is all love, the Grand Master of all brotherhoods, of all churches, all religions, the Lord Christ, clothes himself as a human being like ourselves. He comes down amongst you . . . His presence is with you, in glorious sunlight and truth and wisdom . . . And the eternal and infinite blessing of the Most High pours upon you and fills your heart and soul. Light and joy, comfort and peace . . .

O Lord, may all thy children know that they live and have their being in thee and that only in the consciousness of thy life will they find the true and lasting comforter, the strength and the courage of life.

Amen.

'Judgment'

WE HAVE said before that we in spirit look right into the heart and we know that every man and woman has within them the love of God. We know the goodness of mankind, and we advise you all to seek this goodness in your fellow man, to look for it. This is so often one of the differences between the man in the body of flesh and

129

the man who is free from the entanglements of the flesh and the earth. Train yourselves to look, my brethren, for that spark of light, of God, within your fellows, and approach that – if not verbally then in your heart. To thine own self be true. Be true to God. Be true to your fellow being. If you are true to yourself and to God the Light, you cannot then be false to any man.

It is said that in the world of spirit all is made plain and clear. Now on earth you look as through a dark glass which distorts the soul of man, but when you are released from the body you see face to face, and you see yourself as in a mirror. This, brethren, is the true judgment. In the old days orthodoxy taught you that you would stand before a judge who would condemn you to hell or raise you to heaven. This is the old orthodox Christian teaching. But may we show you what really happens to a man in spirit when he leaves the body and all earthly things? He is very tenderly cared for. He is never judged, nor is he condemned. He is taken eventually into the Temple of the Holy Grail and all around the walls of that temple are mirrors. The man is bidden to look into that mirror, and he sees moving pictures of himself and of his life on earth. He sees himself as he truly is. No one judges him; but he judges himself, because he sees clearly, with sorrow and thankfulness, what he is and how he has behaved in his life on earth.

This is the judgment, this is the moment of choice between 'heaven' or 'hell'; because if this soul accepts in humility the lesson so beautifully shown to him, he sees not only the dark self but also he sees his heavenly self. He recognises his heavenly, his true self. He goes to his heaven not only because he sees the good in himself, but because he sees the good in all his companions. But if he rejects the truth which is being shown him, he himself chooses the darkness which is on the astral plane, where his soul goes for a time.

Now this is what takes place in the spirit spheres. We would say very tenderly to our earthly brethren who seek to live according to the spirit, don't cover your eyes with a blindfold. Have courage, that you may see yourself in very truth. But don't condemn yourself; do not blame yourself. Give yourself love, that is to say, give your lower self love and then you will rise up into the kingdom of God.

Above all, remember to search for God, to search for that spark of light, of divinity, in all peoples. And always see the light developing, the light evolving, the light rising from what appears to be darkness – for out of so-called evil or ignorance good comes.

If you could only put this truth into your life, oh, you would find so much happiness.

'Remission of Sin'

THE CHRISTIAN teaching is that man, if he will only believe on the Lord Jesus Christ, will be redeemed from sin. 'Behold the Lamb of God, which taketh away the sin of the world', and 'the blood of Jesus Christ ... cleanseth us from all sin'. Some of you wince when you hear words such as 'washed in the blood of the Lamb'. You will say, 'But no one believes that in these intellectually enlightened days. All that was in the past. Every thinker today believes that he himself is responsible for his deeds, and it is this personal responsibility for every good or evil deed which will carry the soul into a state of heaven or hell'. It is true; and in spite of the teaching in the New Testament about the blood of the Lamb having the power to remit sins, St Paul said, 'Whatsoever a man soweth, that shall he also reap'. How are we going to harmonise these two apparently contradictory statements? On the one hand we are saved by the shedding of the blood of the Lamb and on the other we are told, 'Whatsoever a man soweth, that shall he also reap'.

Karma is a law of God; and you cannot alter cosmic law. But when the soul has passed through the experience of what you like to call evil or bad karma, it has had its opportunity to pay a debt, remit its sin. The soul can only remit its sin by accepting its own guilt. It is not (as we have

132

formerly supposed) the fact that the Master Jesus was crucified that has redeemed us from our sins. It is the fact that we ourselves in physical life are being crucified by our karma; and because the lower self is purified by the higher self or the Christ self, past sins are washed away.

'Drink', the Master said, 'Take this cup and drink in remembrance of me'. What does this mean, my brethren? That you should drink the cup of human life and human experience, however bitter it may be. Accept it. Learn your lesson of acceptance; for as you take the cup and drink, remembering the Christ in you, your acceptance means that you are being redeemeed by the spirit of Christ that is within. Say, 'In the name of Christ, the supreme light, the perfect Son of God, I accept my karma; I drink the cup, and the life-forces of the Christ fill my whole being and my past errors are washed away'. Why does this cleansing take place? Because with the accepting of the cup, the vision is cleared and the soul sees its past error, and having realised it, experienced it, it is finished.

'The blood of Jesus Christ', said the old-fashioned teaching. But the blood is the life-stream, the wine of life; and you in the sacred sanctuary within the temple of the soul, may take the cup of communion and drink the wine of his life. And you shall be filled with his life and light, there shall be no darkness in you, no fear. His spirit in you triumphs over earth and all its burdens. Live joyously in Christ.

'Saviour' (a Christmas Teaching)

TODAY, many people reject any idea of a saviour of mankind. Man is beginning to assert his individuality and to believe that he can command his fate and thus is his own saviour, that he need not depend upon any other being, however great and good, for his salvation. We would say that he is right in the lesser, but wrong in the greater, deeper sense.

Man's spirit functions through his soul. As man lives, he clothes himself with a body which is called his soul. Soul is not spirit. Spirit is the divine life, the life of God which commences as a seed which grows through incarnation after incarnation, a seed having in itself all the potentialities of a master being. As within the seed or bulb that you plant in springtime lies the subsequent perfection of form, colour and perfume, so in the seed of God planted in man's heart is the promise of the perfect man. But man himself has to make his effort – and this is not easy – the effort always to reach up, to believe, and in time to *know* that love is the king of life and man's saviour.

Although man may reject any idea of a personal saviour, yet through all the ages, through many religions, the same story prevails – of the birth in mysterious circumstances of a teacher, or one who is afterwards called 'saviour'. Such teachers and saviours come to earth to show man the way, to show him how he can save himself. These great ones come into incarnation voluntarily in order to bring the light to mankind at a particular stage on man's evolutionary path. Some people believe that certain astrological aspects draw these souls to earth; but let us remember that not only man, but the planets on their courses, the stars, the suns, are all under the same law of life. Indeed, the whole universe is directed by a supreme divine love – the only word that can describe this overall omnipotence, omniscience and omnipresence. The stars and the planets have an influence, as you all know, upon physical, mental and soul-life, and upon the opportunities which karma brings to the soul in order to hasten its growth and development. The wise men mentioned in the bible were aware that at the birth of Jesus of Nazareth certain planetary influences were at work which brought the opportunity for that holy birth to take place. You see, even in the simple bible story, Jesus was born as a babe in the stable with the animals, indicating the signs of the zodiac, around him. These are just symbols of a heavenly happening; but also of the human spirit born into physical matter, surrounded by signs of the zodiac, through the influence of which it will grow and evolve.

Let us return to the birth of the saviour, the light of God, the Son of God into matter. The saviour is love, love expressed in the form of a man made perfect through love, the highest creation of God, his own counterpart, who comes down to earth and dwells among men.

Jesus was brought up within the brotherhood of the Essenes. He absorbed all their precepts, and adjusted his physical life to their mode of living. He had achieved or attained to his incarnation as Jesus after long, long years in repeated incarnations, preparing his soul-body, his mental body, and higher bodies, to become a perfect instrument for the manifestation of the Lord Christ. You people on earth cannot yet comprehend even a tiny spark of that glory which is the life divine.

The dross which has overlaid the gold is slowly being eliminated. Do you see this? All the wisdom which has been so distorted, all the misunderstandings and the misconceptions which have marred this divine and holy truth of the coming to earth of the Son, will fall away. Shadows will be transmuted and a fresh and clear exposition of the truth will be made known to mankind. This will reveal the true saviour, the real salvation of humanity.

We know the questions which will come. 'Will there be another divine child born who will become a saviour of men even as Jesus did?' you ask. Well, remember that you all live in a materialistic age. The mind has become rampant. Man has become extremely clever, and from childhood onwards has absorbed the opinions of other men, and so the birth of a simple little child like the birth of Jesus would have little effect at present upon the materialistic age. But remember that a great soul *is* drawing near to this earth; and we believe that we are speaking truly when we say that some day a great soul *will* become visible, but only to those who are ready to see and to listen; such developed human souls will certainly see the great one coming in clouds of glorious light. Their eyes will be opened and they will behold the Son of God; but for him to come down a second time into the body of a babe is doubtful, we think. But we are thinking of the raising of the people – 'I, if I be lifted up, from the earth,' said Jesus, 'will draw all men unto me', which means that the spirit of Christ can arise in man's heart. If the spirit of Christ becomes raised, becomes all-powerful, in the lives of the people, then they will behold him as he truly is in that sphere of life which is love, perfection, all service, complete brotherhood, complete harmony, beauty and happiness. This is no fairy tale; this is truth, my brethren, truth.

In the spirit world, when Christmas comes, the outpouring of the Christ spirit is not only upon the earth but upon all the finer spheres above the earth. Then there is great rejoicing.

We assure you that all the joys of the Christ-Mass are truly found in the spirit world. Christmas is a time of great rejoicing, a time of reunion with friends; indeed, the friends in spirit visit their homes on earth and sometimes people are taken to their loved ones in their spirit home. But you see, there is always this 'cutting off' by the earth people of the memory of what they do in spirit. The physical brain does not respond to those waves, those impressions from higher levels of life. So, when you come back, you say: 'No, I can't remember; I don't know anything'.

Well, we are now telling you how to remember. Get to work and train yourselves both by living the life and by your response to God. Train yourselves through meditation, through *knowing* more than by believing.

Never overlook your constant need of remaining calm, tranquil, and still within. You may be active with your hands, doing all kinds of work on the physical plane, to give pleasure to those you love; but in spite of this, deep within you you can keep still and tranquil; you can be at peace; you can look up to the angel throng, catch the mystical spirit of the Christ-Mass. Do not let the noise, clamour and excitement of mind and body overwhelm you. Do not fail to hear heavenly choirs singing out their joy, their praise and their thanksgiving to God for sending to earth the priceless gift of his own Son, his own spirit, to save, to heal, to comfort and to bless.

Open yourselves now to the holy blessing of God, the Father, Mother and Son. Then do our prayers and thanksgiving rise to heaven itself, like incense from the communion table.

Spiritual Discipline

THIS TEACHING was given to a group who had asked for an interpretation of the period, traditional in the orthodox Christian year, of Lent. Although he took this as his starting point, White Eagle gave his theme a far wider compass:

In our simple way, we try to bring you an understanding of the power that is within man, that enables him to liberate himself from the bondage of his mental and physical life. The first necessity is that of becoming still within, tranquil in heart. We may take the simile of a glass of water; if that glass is shaken about the water cannot reflect a true image. It is the same with the human receiver: the brow chakra, the heart chakra must be calm and still if a clear image is to be reflected. This applies not only to an object in the spirit realms of life, but also to truth. To absorb heavenly truth you need to train yourselves in calmness of spirit, calmness of mind. It is not easy for a very active or disturbed mind to receive heavenly truth.

In your Christian year, you have the season which you call Lent. We think the term is derived from an ancient word meaning 'to lengthen'. Lent is the time when the days are beginning to lengthen, when, after the long, dark winter, spring is promised, and Christians look forward to Easter; not so much to the crucifixion, but to that which comes after – the resurrection, the arisen Christ. This is indeed a cause for hope, a glorious anticipation. Let us for a moment in vision see in the heavens not the crucified but the *arisen* Christ, with outstretched arms, glorious in the heart of the blazing Sun; the arisen Christ, Christ the Son of the infinite Father–Mother, the Sun of all life. Let us contemplate that perfect human form. Why should Christ appear in a human form? Has it any meaning for man? Yes; not only as a symbol, but a promise, a demonstration of the truth that man too is a son of God and that man also will arise to the full stature of manhood and Christhood. But before man can arrive at that stage he has to pass through the period called Lent, and during this period he has to sacrifice his desires. These are usually interpreted as physical luxuries and pleasures, which a man denies himself while he strives to devote himself to worship and to prayer.

Now the early Christian groups received instruction from the Great White Brotherhood through their own particular channel of reception;

you too are looking for truth. The truth which you seek is not to be found in any book. The ancient wisdom is rarely printed for all to read. It is unfolded from within man's soul. Help comes to you, as it came to the early Christian brotherhoods, from the Lodge above, from that centre of light where dwell those evolved souls who have passed along the self-same way that you now tread. They have absorbed and have unfolded truth within their own being; and by discipline and work, by service to humanity, have gained mastery over the lower self.

We would not, however, have you choose this path because you wish to gain knowledge and advancement for yourself, but because you cannot follow any other path, because the love of God is burning in your heart. Once you feel such a love, adoration and worship for the divine life, you will receive into your being the power of that life and that light. You have then to learn how to interpret these jewels of spiritual truth in terms of everyday living, in every detail of life. This means that the whole life should be disciplined. We do not say, 'You must'. We gently say, 'My brother, my sister, this discipline, this sacrifice, this overcoming of desire, and the opening of the heart chakra in sweet gentle love to life, is really the only way'. Do not concern yourself with what other people do, perhaps with some of whom you find it difficult to be in harmony. The way to overcome such difficulties is really to set your mind and your thoughts upon God. The only words we can find to explain very simply the way of truth are these: 'Thou shalt love the Lord thy God . . . Thou shalt hold the image or the thought of God ever before thee'.

Now, when once the soul absorbs that spirit, that radiation from the Cosmos, it becomes so imbued with love that the details of everyday life automatically fall into place. For instance, there comes a time when the aspirant foregoes his desires for coarse living, for coarse forms of entertainment, for in the degree that the physical, emotional, desire and mental bodies become purified, sensitised, so do the carnal appetites fall away. In the old days the aspirant was taught to fight the devil. We suggest that the better way is not to fight but to lose interest in the devil by worshipping and loving the good, the true and the beautiful. But you must learn discrimination and discernment, choose your path carefully, and live a *balanced* life. If you practise the art of prayer, of worship, and you open your vision and imagination to the heavenly hosts and breathe into your subtler vehicles the divine light, the sweet breath of heaven, your bodies will become purified. Such purity is essential for the soul who would reflect the perfect life.

So we find that the early Christian brotherhood. taught the need for self-discipline, control of the physical appetites, of the emotions, of the mind, and the strengthening of the spirit during the period you call Lent. In Lent there are forty days. Now, the number forty has an esoteric meaning. The Israelites wandered for forty 'days' in the wilderness, looking for the promised land. A child lies some forty weeks in the womb. The number forty stands for a period of gestation, of waiting, of growth, of development, while the soul who has set his feet upon the path finds itself wandering in the wilderness and has to undergo tests and trials on all planes of being. Thus you see how the period of Lent originated. Nevertheless we do not suggest that you limit the practice of self-discipline to any particular period, but see Lent as symbolic of the training and discipline necessary to the candidate for the heavenly life.

We have spoken of the need for calm and tranquillity of the mind, heart and soul if you would be a reflector of the heavenly life. The soul has to follow a definite path of training, and the initiations, to which we have referred before, are taken steadily through the whole period. The water initiation heralds the controlling, the disciplining of the emotions and desires. The air initiation is the disciplining of the mind and the control of the thoughts. The fire initiation is the disciplining of the great power which at a certain stage is released in man and the wise use of the

143

power of love. Lastly, there is the earth initiation, where the soul learns to surrender everything to the Christ spirit when the lower nature is completely crucified or overcome. Then we behold the arisen Christ, the soul that has freed itself from all material and physical limitations, the soul that is untouchable by the carnal or the fierce emotional desire-nature; and also by the strong mental nature which is the slayer. Remember, my brethren, that the mind of earth is the slayer, inasmuch as it can be over-analytical, harshly critical and cruel. When trained and disciplined through contact with the divine love, then intellect changes into divine intelligence. You know, dear ones, all great souls are very simple, they appear to be childlike, but are full of love, gentleness and sweetness. They know no arrogance. The spirit of love giveth the Christ life. The glorious arisen Christ is born from the heart, not the intellect.

Remember, we have said you have freewill, and it is for you to decide which way you are going. But if you decide to tread the path leading to the glories of heaven, remember you cannot compromise. Having decided, you must abide by your decision and obey the rules or the laws. This means daily watchfulness.

When in your bible Jesus said, 'Watch and pray', it means watch your thoughts, your speech and your daily life. Sometimes you drive yourself into tight corners. Your nervous system cannot support the conditions which you yourself have created. Then you say, 'It is beyond all endurance. Human nature cannot stand it'. No, but it has come about through your own fault. You have not been wise in organising your daily life. Your outer life should never be pushed and rushed around as you people permit it to be, but be governed from the heart. We do not wish you to become over-planned or rigid; what we are advocating is an opening of the heart, and living placidly, quietly, wisely, hour by hour. Do your best; angels in heaven cannot do more. But if you rush and tear about and get excited you are doing no good to yourself or to the world. A slow, ordered path, taken quietly, is best. When you are tempted to rush about, pull yourself up, be still; and you will see how very simply little problems can be solved.

We would emphasise the fact that all you are enduring today is paying off your karma of yesterday, which has to be worked out. You are working it out sometimes by pain and suffering, but the *future* is in your hands. You can control your future during this period of Lent – not necessarily the few weeks before Easter, we are using the word in its universal sense. Here is your opportunity for training, for self-discipline, for control of thought, word and speech. Here is your chance for attunement of life to the purest and highest ideals of cleanliness and purity on every plane of life. You cannot compromise with occult truth. You must be strict and exact, not necessarily with other people, but with yourself.

Perhaps you all know how much better you could do the other person's job, had you the chance. Nevertheless it does not happen to be your job, so concentrate upon your own job so that whatever you do is done to the very best of your ability. Give the other man an occasional word of encouragement. Tell him that he is doing well.

Once you have accepted the path of self-discipline, purity, loving service, gentleness and perfection, then quietly pursue that path. We do not speak of reward; nevertheless, the joy in that life is beyond all earthly understanding. We do not ever say mortify the flesh. We would rather say *glorify* the flesh by the Christ spirit within. We do not agree with the former because the flesh is of God, and the flesh must be glorified by God, by the spirit of the Son of God which is born in flesh.

Early Christian Brotherhoods

IN YOUR scriptures you will read how when a great teacher sought communion with God, sought inspiration from God, he went up into a mountain. Moses when called by God ascended Mount Sinai, and there received the Commandments. Jesus went up into a mountain and when he was set his disciples came, and he opened his mouth and taught them. All Masters first of all raise the consciousness of their pupils. Pupils cannot remain on the level of earth; they rise into a higher state of consciousness. Only at that higher level can heavenly truth be perfectly received.

This is what the early Christians were taught. The early Christian brotherhoods received deep teaching from their Master and his helpers, the elder brethren. Of course much of this has been lost with time. These early brethren of the Christ-circle knew of the truth of the ancient wisdom; they knew and understood and practised what might be called reincarnation, the law of cause and effect; they understood esoteric spiritualism. They understood about the subtler bodies of man. They understood how through meditation and aspiration and good brotherly deeds they could unfold their inner spiritual gifts. They knew how through their life of service and worship they could stimulate and open their chakras and use their inner gifts for the blessing of mankind. They knew that there was no death; that when the body had finished its work, it was discarded; but that they themselves were just the same. Although simple, these men had a deep occult knowledge which only a few retain today. In later times these holy men were sometimes forced underground, and had to hold their meetings in caves and hidden places for fear of persecution.

Now these great truths of life are still there for man to find for himself, when he has once learned and can obey the law of holy and pure living and loving his fellow creatures – not only his fellows but his fellow-creatures of the animal, the nature kingdom, and all life. He raises his vibrations through love. He aspires to and receives inspiration from heaven. The hosts in the Christ-circle are ever on the look-out for those whom they can help. Oh, so eagerly and happily do they come to you from this sphere of Christ. The mistake that so many people make is to think, 'Oh, God is up there and we are down here. The angels are in the heavens; we are too dark and too bad for them to reach us'. True humility does not believe such things. God's angels have learned how to love divinely. They come to the lowliest on earth, if those lowly ones cry out in truth and sincerity; 'Oh, Lord, I want to do good and I want to be good. Help me to be like thee'. Then the angels hasten. An earnest and sincere cry from the heart brings the winged messenger at once.

We would leave you with a vision of the heavens above and around you, and of the outpouring of the divine rays upon the earth; of the future stimulation in man of all the Godlike qualities and faculties; and with this, the illumination of the earth, and the salvation through the Son of God of the soul of the earth and of mankind.

You can work out for yourselves what this illumination means if you consider what life could be like if the divine laws of living were obeyed, and if every man, woman and child became as clear and bright as is a true Son of God. Think of the harmony and beauty of the earth, then try to imagine what the spirit world is like. In the spheres of light men go about in tranquillity of spirit, with shining God-like faces. Every piece of work is executed perfectly, and the effort of all is applied to further the happiness of the community. Always in your inner selves and in your quiet moments you can rise into this perfect life, and receive from those who dwell there the inspiration to live likewise on the earth. Don't make the excuse that man is only human. With all the force of the truth that is in us, we say, we know, that man is divine. May his divinity become supreme.

IX

In the Aquarian Age

IN THIS CHAPTER we print two teachings which in different ways look forward to the Aquarian Age.

All are of the Same Spirit

BELOVED brethren, we are all of the same family, of the same spirit. Whoever we are, whatever we are, either spiritually or physically, we are brethren in the one spirit; we are all children of the heavenly Father and the great Mother, and we are the younger brethren of the great Masters of all time, and of all those sainted souls who have helped humanity along the path of spiritual evolution. We would suggest that our earthly brethren should remember this ancient way of prayer: each day remember with reverence the heavenly Father and the spiritual spheres around you; remember the gift of your physical life from the great Mother of all form; and remember the ancient ones and those advanced beings who come to the earth to assist humanity to climb the ladder from the earth to the golden city of Jerusalem.

If you study the various known religions, you will find that they all present truth in parables, but parables which seem to contradict each other, and this causes a good deal of confusion. But you will notice that as mankind evolves, a tendency will grow for the differences between sects and religions to be resolved; there will be moves towards unity, and a growing desire to be tolerant towards another's religion. From the world of spirit comes the urge to allow other people, other nations, other religions, to follow their way of life, and through following this urge man is getting drawn nearer and nearer to the centre of the circle. All religions are like spokes of a wheel, or rays of light, all radiating from the hub of that wheel, which is the Great White Spirit, the heavenly Father, the eternal and infinite Father of all mankind.

What is truly called the ancient wisdom is the teaching from the centre of the hub of the wheel, the teaching of the spirit which flows from the hub of the wheel and runs along these spokes or these different channels of religious thought right to the outermost. The inner teaching is the teaching of the inner life of the spirit, given to humanity by the sages, the God-men of all time. But you have to remember that this teaching of the spirit was given in symbols or in parables suitable to the particular nation or state of development of humanity. But what happens, and what

151

will always happen until man is assured of his own inner being, is that the lower or frontal mind interprets these teachings according to the level of the mind at that particular state of development. Thus in time confusion arises, .truth becomes distorted, and wrong ideas are presented to the people. If you will remember this, it will help you to develop the quality of discernment.

All esoteric teaching springs from one source of truth.

We would like you to see this truth as a tree – a tree of knowledge, shall we call it? planted in the infinite and eternal garden. That tree has many branches, big branches breaking up into smaller branches and even smaller and smaller, down to the smallest twig. These branches are all aspects of esoteric truth and they are innumerable. But man gets hold of one branch or one little twig and thinks he has the whole truth and that his truth is the only truth. By so doing he is enclosing himself in a little dark box which we will call the mind, and it can become a very dark prison.

But the time comes when man is touched in his heart by the love of God. And so we come back to our first words to you: he may express that love in many ways before he realises that the love he is feeling must extend to all creation. When he feels this, he is beginning to awaken, however slowly, to the realisation of the infinite and eternal love of God. He begins to realise that

the light of the spirit is the Son of the heavenly
parents, Father and Mother, and that his body is
only an instrument for this divine Son.

In the Aquarian Age

MAN COMES forth from the heart of God without
consciousness of his true nature; during his age-
long experience, through which he is gradually
becoming God-conscious, he has been building
those subtle bodies, such as his emotional body,
and his mental body, which now he is using.

Man has now reached the outermost manifestation in the dense matter of this earth plane,
for with the development of his fine intellect it
would appear that he has reached his limit of
involution. Now he turns his face upwards; having
touched the depths, he faces now the upward arc
on his return to God.

In the Aquarian Age man will become conscious
of his real nature. Some of you who feel you
have attained a little knowledge look about you
and wonder if your brethren have any spiritual
quality at all, so governed by lower instincts and
desires do they seem, so far removed from the
angelic.

Don't judge too harshly. When you look upon
apparent darkness and conflict, selfishness and
violence, try to see that which grows within; see
the seed struggling to break through its hard

153

sheath, a seed struggling for expression through the density of earth. The Aquarian Age will bring a tremendous outpouring from the spiritual Sun onto the earth to quicken that seed lying in the darkness – such energy and light as you cannot at present comprehend. At the time of the crucifixion of Jesus, a vital spirit was released. This was a world baptism in which all participated, but it has taken ages (according to your understanding) for this vital body of the Sun to permeate the particles or atoms of the physical self of man. Nevertheless within your own vital body flows a life-giving stream from the vital body of the Christ.

We would rather create the picture of a glorious and continual growth taking place in humanity. In the Aquarian Age this consciousness of the living Christ will gradually increase in man. Then there will be no more shedding of blood, no more separation and strife, but an intermingling of all planes of spiritual life (symbolised by the rending of the temple veil at the time of the crucifixion of Jesus). Men will open their eyes to see the glories of heaven; there will be no more separation, no more tears. The sorrow and sickness which afflict mankind will be overcome; for by the resurrection of the Christ within, man will have entered into the kingdom of God and all his limitations will have passed away.

154